The SERMON MAKER

TALES

OF A

TRANSFORMED

PREACHER

The SERMON MAKER

TALES

OF A

TRANSFORMED

PREACHER

CALVIN MILLER

ZONDERVAN™

GRAND RAPIDS, MICHIGAN 49530 USA

ZONDERVAN™

The Sermon Maker
Copyright © 2002 by Calvin Miller

Requests for information should be addressed to:
Zondervan, *Grand Rapids, Michigan 49530*

Library of Congress Cataloging-in-Publication Data

Miller, Calvin.
     The sermon maker : tales of a transformed preacher / Calvin Miller.
       p. cm.
     ISBN 0-310-25509-0 (softcover)
      1. Clergy — Fiction.   2. Preaching — Fiction.   I. Title.
    PS3563.I376 S47 2002
    813'.54 — dc21

                                                2002000786

Published in association with the literary agency of Alive Communications, Inc., 7680 Goddard Street, Suite 200, Colorado Springs, CO 80920.

Interior design by Beth Shagene

Printed in the United States of America

03 04 05 06 07 08 09 /❖ DC/ 10 9 8 7 6 5 4 3 2

CONTENTS

THE ARENA OF LIFE

All forms of communication are always being modified by those they serve. Not long ago I attended a pastor's conference and was struck again by the way that preaching styles often remain tied to past forms. Why? Because preachers have not asked themselves often enough, "How do contemporary audiences listen?" Many of the sermons I heard at the conference were strong on exegesis—and they should be. They were strong on what is generally called expository style—and they should be. But as I listened, I imagined myself sitting in an audience one hundred years ago. Oddly, everything fit. In fact, it seemed to fit most of the last century better than this one. The sermons were void of references to the age in which we now live. This was particularly true of those preachers who had a heavy precept outline style and used no current illustrations in conjunction with the ancient text.

Biblical truth is timeless. But the way each generation hears and appropriates truth is quite different. There are at least four major translations of the Bible between us and the Bible writers: into Greek, into Latin, into Elizabethan English, into modern English. Why translate at all? Because language is fundamental to communication. It's how we gather information.

The midtwentieth century produced a shift from the industrial age to the age of information. Jeremy Rifkin called this shift the "emerging order." Alvin Toffler referred to it as the "third wave." Neil Postman called it a passing from the age of print to the age of image. It is Postman's wise observation, especially in his *Amusing Ourselves to Death*, that bids the pulpit move from verbally driven sermons to image-driven sermons.

However you label our current postmodern, postliberal, post-denominational world, preaching today must be postprecept. In a video-driven world, the wise preacher will learn to preach in ways that lets the image do the talking.

Modern communications theorists agree that our brave new world hears best in megabytes of reason. A thirty-minute sermon divided into three ten-minute points is not as effective as a thirty-minute sermon divided into ten three-minute points. These three minutes David Buttrick calls structures. We move the sermon's contents better when we unload it in smaller packages. Yet the sermons one hears at many evangelical pastor's conferences still follow the older three-point model.

Most people hear stories better than they hear megabytes of truth framed in point-driven logic. Perhaps this is why Jesus used them so often. Yet many preachers still seem addicted to a plodding, logic-driven methodology. Metaphor is often entirely missing from such sermons, yet every modern communications specialist agrees that we both "think and store" in mental pictures.

The myth still persists among many evangelicals that biblical exposition is precept only. To left-brain expositors, stories are not exposition, and to suggest that they are is to be "liberal." In every homiletics class I teach there will usually be at least one student who says, "Do you preach expository sermons or do you tell stories?" I remind them that Jesus told stories and was a master of exposition. This usually quiets all but those who suffer from massive pulpit trauma and homiletic dysfunction.

This book sets out to address these communication foibles. I realize that many of the most popular preaching books are always titled something like *Basic Expository Preaching* and are subtitled *How to Preach Biblical Sermons with the Aid of the Holy Spirit to Motivate People to Salvation*. I ask you to trust me that our values are one in this matter. Could we simply take the importance of exposition for granted? This book will indeed be aimed at helping us preach biblical sermons with the help of the Holy Spirit. It does not ignore the fact that we should dig around with Hebrew and Greek word studies and the insights of various commentaries. These things always have been and always will be a part of good sermon study.

I have written this book with many notes, to provide the reader with good information on preaching. These notes are not necessary to the stories, which stand on their own. But the notes can furnish the mind with strong arguments on the subject of sermon preparation. Some readers might prefer to ignore the notes during a first reading of the stories in order to better enjoy them without interruption, then go back and reread the stories, this time also reading the notes as they come to them. Others might find it easy enough to read the notes while reading the stories the first time through. One could even read the stories without the notes and then go back and read the notes without the stories. Read it whatever way works best for you.

In this book I have set out to achieve a simple task: to consider how we can marry exposition and metaphor in such a way that people will listen. Most preaching books I pick up are books on how to write sermons. This one is about how people hear them.

Calvin Miller
Birmingham, Alabama

ONE

THE PASSION
AND THE CALL

Pastor Sam was tired. Monday tired. He felt as
though he had been skewered on the white spire of his
church. He was only in his thirties, but he felt old ...
very old. He groaned a little in remembering he was now
too old for the chaplaincy. It was one of those Mondays
when he sometimes sang "Be not dismayed whate'er
betide, God will take care of you" and sometimes "Don't
nobody bring me no bad news."

Emma Johnson was waiting for Sam just inside his
office.

Emma ... no, Lord, not Emma, begged Sam in silent
desperation when he saw her. But to ask that Emma not
be in his office was like asking God to make St. Louis the
capital of Missouri. It was not going to happen. There
she was. Emma! Emma! Deep-set eyes, an aquiline nose,
and a Jeffersonian chin. Proud, stiff of spine, white

1. We all attend churches and listen to sermons because we are hungry for some renovation of the Spirit. We actually hunger to be made better. We suspect sermons can help us with this, and we are ready for the help. James L. Crenshaw writes:

> Surely, we can identify with these people. Fearing extinction, we freeze our bodies and build storm shelters and space shuttles. Who among us does not breathe the air of ambition, has not drunk the heady wine of desire to achieve something truly extraordinary—even if only in our secret daydreams? We kill ourselves making bricks, meeting deadlines, and for what purpose? In the end, God will come down, and our puny anthills will be washed away with the next light sprinkle.[1]

We are all aware that this can happen only when sermons get rough with our buoyant egos. In some ways, modern hymns and choruses spend the first part of a worship service causing us to congratulate ourselves on our encounter with grace. Then comes an honest sermon! There we must take all of our self-esteem—the healthy and the unhealthy—and subject it to the harder work of the sermon: the work of scraping and scouring our unhealthy pride.

orthopedic hose, and brown Cuban heels. She was a relic left over from the cold war, a Balkan weight lifter who carried a Bible big enough to frighten a Texas evangelist. Sincere and stout she was—and the oracle of God's will for Sam's life. *Lord, I have the faith to remove a mountain and cast it into the depths of the sea*, prayed Sam, *but please . . . help Emma to be kind.*

But his prayer of hope died when Emma said, "Sam, I may not be the one to tell you this, but I feel that God has specifically told me to tell you your preaching is boring."

There it was, the hand against the plaster—*MENE, MENE, TEKEL, UPARSIN*—Sam's sermon judgment was on the very wall where his hide would soon be nailed.

"Gosh, Emma, thanks. One can never get enough good constructive criticism, so don't hold back; please tell me how you really feel."

"All right! If you insist, Sam. Preaching exists to get things done. It exists to help people catch a new view of their lives. It serves to help people understand who God is and what he expects of them. Preaching should not be namby-pamby; it should overwhelm people with the truth it tells, and it should overturn their little lives with great new images of who they are and what God expects of them."[1]

"Emma, could we talk about this later . . . maybe next August?"

2. Sermons become boring as they lose their homiletic nature. *Homily* has to do with conversation, and conversation is dialogue. Dialogue means two heads locked in the enchantment of relationship. Sermons lose their force over listeners at the same rate at which they become boring. Sermons were never intended to be one man alone piloting some supersonic exegesis. Sermons are a squadron of need—pastor and people all flying in formation and talking together about the flight, even as they fly. John Stott observes:

> What is needed today then is the same synthesis of reason and emotion, exposition and exhortation, as was achieved by Paul.[2]

This statement is fine, but it ignores one of the most important aspects of preaching: relationship! Sermons don't have a *raison d'être* until they understand that good exposition alone cannot create interest. Homiletics is truth set between two minds, both of which have equal interest in it.

"Well, I never . . ." she began but didn't finish what it was that she never would do. Her eyes narrowed to slits and lasered a hole through Sam's dyspepsia.

She turned on her Cuban heels and walked briskly away. The little curls on the side of her head bobbed up and down in wrath. She was clearly offended. Sam felt scathed by her frequent revelations from the Lord. Why did God never give her anything nice to pass on to him? She was Sam's apocalyptic angel, ever harping on his weaknesses and trampling out the grapes of wrath.

Still, Sam's whole life seemed to be on hold. His preaching was not going all that well, and Emma's stern sermon appraisal had convinced him that the angels were on her side and not his. He felt it had been a long time since he had preached any great sermons. He knew he could never "bless her socks off," as the youth minister would say, but if only he could preach her into culottes and pretty patent-leather pumps, maybe the Spirit would fall in wind and fire. Still, he had to admit that Emma's word "boring" had often come to mind as he preached. He *was* boring, even to himself. It was the last and most lamentable state of preachers.[2] Sam felt there was no feeling worse than knowing your sermon was boring as you were preaching it. It was horror to know your homiletic plane was going down in flames and you were in the cockpit trying to land it where the wreckage wouldn't hurt anyone. If there was anything worse than laying an egg in the pulpit on

3. Sermons take their life from the nearness of God. When God is present in the document, he will also be present in the preacher's life. All worshipers to one degree or another desire a greater level of intimacy with God. Given the slightest hope that God has anything to say to them, they will listen ardently. They listen out of the desperate hope that the preacher possesses a greater level of intimacy than they themselves do.

Perhaps that's why evangelistic preaching holds a high level of interest. Those who hear an inflamed soul speaking warmly of Jesus are convinced that the speaker's level of intimacy is what they want for themselves. Keith Willhite says:

> This is where relevant, biblical preaching begins, continues, and ends; from the specifics of and making exegetical decisions or "I need an illustration," all the way through to praying that my heart will be right before God as I preach and that people will come prepared to hear and do the Word of God. There is absolutely no substitute for prayer and the power of the Holy Spirit in preaching.[3]

This intimate Jesus always appears near at hand working all kinds of miracles in the lives of those who really need to hear from him.

Sunday, it was having Emma serve it to you scrambled on Monday.

But how had *boring* come to be Sam's adjective?

Sam had been out of seminary for only seven years. Now he had begun to wonder where all those feelings he once had for God had gone. He could remember, somewhere—way back before his graduation, far beyond his arrival at his first church—that his old homiletics professor had said, "It is not possible to preach a vital sermon about God when God is somewhere beyond us, out past the borders of our everyday lives."[3]

Back then, the statement seemed academic. He had first run into the idea in seminary. But then, seminary was the place for academic statements. You really didn't need to know how to relate in seminary; you only had to talk about how to relate.

But now Sam couldn't afford to be academic. He was fighting for his very life. His sermons were boring. God must have been the first to notice it. Now he knew it. Worst of all, Emma knew it. God, being compassionate, would tell no one, but Emma was quite different from God in these matters.

But why was Sam boring? He was working hard to make his sermons interesting. He was always "on the make" for a great quote, a fascinating word study, a powerful set of statistics, a refreshing insight from some other preacher's boring cassette. He kept telling himself that if he worked hard enough on such things, preaching would get easier. But try as

4. When preachers lose track of God, their sermons get pushier. Not only that, when God is most absent in their lives, they are all the more present. The quieter God gets, the louder they get.

Barbara Brown Taylor raises this same issue:

> Sometimes I think we do all the talking because we are afraid God won't. Or, conversely, that God will. Either way, staying preoccupied with our own words seems a safer bet than opening ourselves up either to God's silence or God's speech, both of which have the power to undo us.[4]

So we lose God when he's quiet, because we're too loud. We run from him when he gets loud, because we cannot stand the storm of his coming. Either way, we often come to the pulpit without him, having no clear remembrance of our last real conversation.

he might, he had not been able to come up with any kind of sermon preparation that would make a sermon really work for him. Everything he wrote looked good on paper but felt wooden when he read it out loud.

Sam couldn't help feeling that the reason for his boring homilies was that he had lost something more important than mere sermon preparation. He had laid by something more fundamental. He had lost the rapport he once felt with God. There was a hole in the center of his relationship with God. He needed back that old zeal he had mislaid. But try as he might, he just had no idea where he had mislaid it and therefore no idea how to pick it up again.[4]

The week moved on. Tuesday was nicer to Sam. It was always nicer than Monday. Tuesday gave Sam reason to hope. Emma didn't come; God seemed compassionate. Wednesday was better than Tuesday, Thursday than Wednesday, and so on. Then dawned Saturday! Next to Monday, Saturday was the dark day of the week. Saturday was the day when sermons wouldn't finish themselves. When preachers doubted. Saturdays and Mondays were Sundays' bookends. On Saturday preachers were neurotic planning what they would say, and on Monday they were neurotic for having said it.

On Saturday evening Sam took his usual stroll through the empty sanctuary. The room seemed warm and friendly. Then he looked at the place where Emma would sit to grade his sermon. Emma's pew! His stomach knotted. He reached

19

5. Great communication is based on liking our audience rather than fearing them. Bill Hybels lists two essentials for audience analysis:

> The first is to *understand the way they think*. . . . The second prerequisite to effective preaching to non-Christians is that we *like them*.[5]

We can never speak to people while we fear them.

I suspect this is why paralyzing nervousness is an unhealthy homiletic pathology. While we try to speak in bondage to our fears, we will find ourselves so concerned with our terror that we eliminate the audience altogether. Fear forces us into egotistic quaking, and once we agree to be afraid of people, they cease to exist. We then become so self-concerned that God himself also leaves us, for we have become so ego intensive that only our phobias define us. With God and the audience both gone, all we can do is succumb to our madness and quake.

6. Way back in 1877, Phillips Brooks made this observation in his Yale lectures: "Some men are made for manuscripts, and some for the open platform."[6]

Some preachers get along well with pulpits; some feel bound by them. Preaching must be free of all artificial constraints. If pulpits imprison a preacher, they should be made smaller or banished if necessary. But the heaviest of pulpits disappear under the freedom of a great pulpit style. The point is this: if the audience notices that the preacher is captive to the pulpit, the sermon is not free. They may not know why the sermon is bound up by the pulpit, but they will be able to see that it is.

in his pocket for the roll of antacids that had become nearly as essential as his notes in preaching. He imagined the church full of people. There were two things which actually frightened him. The people and the pulpit. It was a recipe for terror.

Why was he so afraid of the people of his parish? When they were sick or in the hospital, they welcomed him as a kind of physician who would bless them with prayer and wisdom. When he met them at wedding rehearsals, they gave him cake and punch and seemed altogether civil. When he visited them in their homes, they were downright gracious. But when they filled the hardwood pews on Sunday, they were a giant jury handing him his life sentence of doing time in the pulpit.[5]

Sam wanted to instruct them. He wanted to enlighten them, to inform them, to make them wise in the ways of the Bible. But no matter how much he dedicated himself to this task, they always seemed to be camped across the universe.

Over the recent months, Sam's audience fears had come to focus on the pulpit. Pulpits were fearsome furniture indeed.[6] They called those who stood behind them to appear to be patriarchs and prophets lately descended from the presence of the Almighty. Sam hated the image because he felt he could never live up to it. If the pulpit was there to change him into Amos or Jeremiah or Isaiah, it failed. It only made him all the more aware that those who were arrogant enough to stand behind the sacred desk immediately labeled themselves

incompetent. Who could, by merely standing behind a box, be transformed into an otherworldly oracle of God? Here preachers were to gird up their insecurities and say "Presto! *Kerusso*" and be changed from a mewling minister to a nuclear Nehemiah, fearless and fiery.

The whole idea was to thump the box, speak for God, and remain a real human being. Did Elijah go through this? How does any preacher wind up such a blend of acid and aspartame, Amos of Tekoa and Schuller of Garden Grove? When a preacher is too much a fiery prophet, children won't sit by him at casserole dinners. When he is too much a human being, they won't trust him to explain the Revelation to them. He must speak with the authority of Kittel and yet be conversant in the Second Coming novels his people all read.

But Sam's particular pulpit was a bad place to think well of himself. Sam stopped in the darkness and studied the pulpit. It was an oaken obscenity! "It always demanded so much more of me than I could ever deliver," Sam said aloud. He said it so aloud that he felt a twinge of fear that someone—the janitor or some unexpected parishioner—might have overheard his lament. But the sanctuary was quiet. And so he stood and faced the pulpit, studying it, scrutinizing it, measuring it.

It was called the MacArthur pulpit.

It had a little brass plate that read, "Given by the friends of George MacArthur, in loving memory." The plate, however, was all that was little about it. The pulpit itself was a

7. One of the worst things large pulpits do is block visibility. To some extent, the more of a preacher people can see, the better he or she will be heard. Pulpits can hide the preacher's gestures and limit his movement. Why is this bad? Because movement is always more interesting than a stolid style. To be sure, too much movement can be distracting. But well-planned movement can add the grace of interest to the laws of good exegesis. Willhite writes:

> Moreover, be sure that the gesture matches your words. If you choose the word "huge," but hold your hands only shoulder-width apart, the gesture distracts.
>
> A second aspect of nonverbal communication that can increase clarity is the use of physical movement to establish your main points.[7]

Postmodern church attendees prefer movement. When passion really drives the sermon, the energy should not be hidden behind an overlarge pulpit. Socrates said that in speech, the body speaks too. This *sermo corporis* should not be hidden. The energy of the sermon acts to compel the audience. It must be seen as well as heard.

battleship. Made of solid oak, its heavy moldings descended eastward and westward in impregnable battlements. Every sermon preached behind it seemed smaller than it was. When the sermons were strong, its liturgical lumber seemed to shout, "See, I told you so!" When the sermons were poor, the pulpit's haughty hardwood railed against Sam's weak oratory and sneered upon his littleness.

Sam preached from this mighty fortress, born fifty years before him when the Matterhorn had mated with a logging truck. He wearied of its almighty carpentry. To really be heard, he had to out-shout the lumber that stood between himself and his needy people. To be seen, he had to walk to the side of it. But whichever way Sam moved, it was a long walk. Its central bulwark stood four feet, seven inches tall. But its remaining towers fell off in wing walls that left the whole frigate six centimeters short of paralysis.

It was Fort Wilderness with a cross on it.

It was the Titanic of God, unsinkable, eternal.

But oh, was it steadfast![7]

It was just the place for God's Word. It never lied. And it never told the truth quietly. It always thundered, frightening sinners into confession and numbing little children into peeping out from behind their parents to have a fearful peek at God. Sam wished it smaller, but it had been given to the church by Emma's grandparents shortly after World War I, in honor of George MacArthur, who had died in the service.

8. Pulpits are places where our ordinary preaching phobias are magnified. We face the sermon place terrified of grace. Why? Because we cannot imagine how we will be received. Hugh Litchfield expresses our fear of the pulpit:

> I meet quite a number of ministers who do not particularly like to preach. Standing to speak before a group of people is frightening to them. I relate to that. I have a love/hate relationship with preaching. I love it because I feel it is what God has called me to do. Also, to have the privilege to preach the good news of the gospel is a blessing. But I hate it because it is not easy to do. Maybe I'll forget! Maybe they won't like what I say![8]

Why do we stand up and go on with it?
Because God wants it done.

9. Of all the scary notions that preaching engenders, it must be that we both write and deliver sermons in the presence of angels. The idea that our mortal clay could be capable of working with a transcendent God really terrifies us.

All men of faith are asked to live with the unreasonable demands of an unreasonable God. In William Golding's novel *The Spire*, Golding examines what God asked of Noah, Hosea, and Abraham:

> Even in the old days He never asked men to do what was reasonable. Men can do that for themselves. They can buy and sell, heal and govern. But then out of some deep place comes the command to do what makes no sense at all—to build a ship on dry land; to sit among the dunghills; to marry a whore; to set their son on the altar of sacrifice. Then, if men have faith, a new thing comes.[9]

So when God moves in and we hear the brush of angel wings, we tremble. Yet without the involvement of a transcendent God, sermons are at best speeches and at the worst pointless.

Even as Sam looked at the pulpit, he felt inadequate. In less than fifteen hours he would have to stand behind the wood and preach the sermon that was lying on his desk. He fell to his knees in the empty sanctuary and said, "Miserere Domine!"[8]

Sam felt a sudden flood of terror. He was not alone! Someone was kneeling beside him. He looked up, startled. He was terrified.

"Excuse me," Sam said, breathing in heavy terror, "but do I know you?"

"Not yet!"

Sam struggled to his feet. His surprise visitor pulled him back down.

"Sam, don't get up. You look good on your knees! It's a healthy sign in the land where I'm from. My boss has been concerned that you haven't been on your knees enough. It's the best place to begin a sermon, you know."

"Who is your boss?"

"He's your boss too. We have the same boss. Let me introduce myself. I've come to pay you a call of mercy. Believe it or not I'm—"

"An angel?" Sam gasped.[9]

Now he could see that the intruder had huge feathery wings arching above his shoulders. It was so uncanny, Sam wanted to laugh, but the severity of the intruder's countenance made Sam retreat behind a wall of questions. "Well what kind

10. Why is there a distinct terror in preaching? Because the task of speaking for God is ever bigger than we are. Barbara Brown Taylor speaks of the terror in this way:

> Last year I complained in writing to a friend that I was not sure people even listened to sermons anymore. She wrote back, "I do think people are trying to listen and that preaching does matter. In fact, I think the vast majority of people are sitting in the pews with parched lips. They are so thirsty that they have lost their ability to listen, to speak, or to think."[10]

What an image. The world is thirsty. It's our job to get them to drink before their thirst destroys them. No wonder we are terrified. If we cannot entice them to the water of life, God will not—at least for the moment—be able to do much for our own particular corner of his thirsty planet.

of angel are you? Are you Raphael, Michael, Gabriel, Uriel, or Hazael? Are you one of the seven archangels?"

"Actually, I'm the eighth archangel," said the intruder. "I'm Sermoniel, the Angel of Homiletics. I go around helping powerless preachers get it back."

"Get what back?"

"Come, come, man! You don't mean to tell me you are still pretending you have no second thoughts about your effectiveness? Preaching is much more than you ever bargained for, isn't it? It's rough out there, isn't it? There behind the big box is where you stand alone, strengthened only by God. There you hang your every word out in the open. Anybody can shoot it down. It's the loneliest, cussedest, blessedest work in the world.[10]

"Have you not felt the terror of preaching? The death sweat in the palms of your hands, the clench in the intestines, the gelatin in your joints, the lock-up in your larynx, the tonnage of the tongue, the ice in your arteries, the drain of the adrenalin, the mental muck, the—"

"Yes! Stop! I know all these things. These are the demons who share my nest. I just don't know what to do about them."

"Well relax, man! I'm your personal guardian, your angel of homiletic therapy! You have a condition known as sermonic sclerosis, or hardening of the homily. We call it by its more Latin name, homileticus horribilis. It is terminal. Most preachers die of it long before they are boxed and

11. Preaching unheard sermons is never the fault of the listener; it is the fault of the communicator. Yet Spurgeon was right: to preach to the snoring must be wretched work.

> *The twenty-day sermon*
> *Of Reverend Tom Herman*
> *Began on a Sunday*
> *And lasted three weeks.*
> *And nobody stayed*
> *Till the sermon was done.*
> *When God came to town,*
> *The Reverend Tom Herman*
> *Invited God over*
> *To hear Herman speak,*
> *But God replied, "Tom,*
> *I can't stay that long;*
> *I'm only in town for the week."*[11]

Even God, it would seem, has little time for sermons that don't matter.

buried. In fact, most preachers go on preaching for years after people quit listening . . . You know what I mean?"

Sam nodded. He knew.

"The Boss keeps an account of one poor preacher who still holds the world's record for the most sermons preached after absolutely everyone quit listening. He preached for thirty-two years after all interest in his sermons ceased.[11] He died preaching in an empty sanctuary, apparently unaware it was empty. It's possible to get so sermon-centered you never think of the crowd. Anyway, it was a couple of weeks before anyone found him. He had rigor mortis something awful. He was so stiff they were barely able to fold him up and get him in a box. Not surprising, though. Rigor mortis goes with sermonic sclerosis."

"Is it always terminal?"

"No, that's why I've come to you. It's latent; you can get rid of it, or at least you can live on top of it. You're young enough that if you work at it you could actually see it go into remission."

"How?"

"Well, Sam, there's good news and bad news."

"Give me the good news first," said Sam.

"Fine," said Sermoniel. "You can be healed of homileticus horribilis."

"How?"

12. To be healed of that sermonic deadness demands that we open our eyes to see who we really are. We are weak little gulls set against the thunderheads of transcendence. We are the spin doctors whose thin logic is too small a paddle to stir the thick mysteries of the Spirit. As long as we remember God's greatness and our foolishness, we may be healed of our sermonic deadness. James Crenshaw writes:

> In each of us rests a little bit of biblical character. At times we act like second-generation Christians who have never brushed against mystery. Our lives are wholly ordinary, characterized by trivia, devoid of transcendence, wholly this-worldly. Thus we cannot confirm the truth of what our ancestors have affirmed. At other times we face mystery with sheer terror, for we know our frame.[12]

Preachers who are so dead that they hold no possibility of life may be those who actually believe they are good speakers in charge of their careers.

13. Here's to mediocrity! Who does not love it? To be average and content with it holds its own damnation. To be average: what is it?

> *The best of the worst*
> *The worst of the best*

To be average is to camp out eating marshmallows halfway between significance and insignificance. It is to avoid the dangers of extremism by snuggling down in the middle of the masses. John Piper tells us that the comfortable and mediocre are flippant about God and probably don't care too much about people. Kenton Anderson writes:

> There is a kind of popular, cultural relativism that enables people to dispense flippantly with uncomfortable biblical teaching. Where these kind of things take root, the Bible will be silenced in the church.[13]

But then, why wouldn't it be so? Those who never strive to be better will have little that is good to say.

"That's the bad news! Overcoming the condition means that you must redefine the source of the sermon."[12]

"The source?"

"Yes. Great sermons don't merely spring from good homiletic practice. They don't come from tons of study. Study can inform the sermon, but it cannot teach it its music. It can make a sermon walk, but it will never furnish it with wings. It's a common flaw among preachers to believe that if they work hard at exegesis and the commentaries, they will become vibrant, fascinating preachers. Of course, all sermonic tools have their place in sermon preparation, but great preaching grows only from the soil of great lives."

"Great lives? Then I can never do it. Great lives? That's an overwhelming idea. Who could ever be a great person or live a great life? The world breeds mediocrity. But that's where I live and I love it. I'm not afraid of it. I'm comfortable with it."[13]

"That's a bad attitude, Sam. Mediocrity is the prison of the timid. Greatness is arrived at by the unflinching pursuit of great ideals. Greatness of spirit results from our passions, our drive to care about something supremely important."

"Something important?"

"Yes, some *thing*, or some *one*, important."

"But how can I ever arrive at this kind of concern?"

"It's not how you arrive there; it's a matter of returning there. Sam, you had it once. Almost all preachers have it to

14. The call is both mysterious and important. Those who have it are at a loss often to define it. Those who don't aren't sure what they are missing. Os Guinness defines it in these words:

> Answering the call of our Creator is "the ultimate why" for living, the highest source of purpose in human existence. Apart from such a calling, all hope of discovering purpose (as in the current talk of shifting "from success to significance") will end in disappointment. To be sure, calling is not what it is commonly thought to be. It has to be dug out from under the rubble of ignorance and confusion. And, uncomfortably, it often flies directly in the face of our human inclinations. But nothing short of God's call can ground and fulfill the truest human desire for purpose.[14]

Perhaps all of this is to say that the call is that for which we can die. Knowing what we will die for gives us the primary clue as to what we should live for.

15. We must journey to the edge of heat if we would catch the flame. When Blaise Pascal died in 1662, his servant found a scrap of paper hidden in the lining of his coat. It turned out to be a testimony of something that had happened eight years earlier: "From about half past ten in the evening until about half past twelve FIRE . . ."[15]

Whatever happened to him that Monday night, "FIRE" was all Pascal could say about it. For two whole hours, nothing but fire. Not the fire of philosophers and scholars but the fire of God. And when the fire has burned through us, our passion is the evidence that we are aflame with significance.

begin with. That's how most preachers get into the ministry. They are swept up in a call, an all-enmeshing idea that is bigger than themselves.[14] In some despondent turn of the screw, they bump into grace. They find themselves prisoners of the force of love. They collide with God in a headlong romance of purpose. They are possessed with an incredible lightness of being. They swim a gilded stream that defies their description of it. God is! He loves! He is love! The world is needy and God needs help to inform the dull planet that he is crazy about the human race."

Sermoniel paused.

Sam shifted from his knees and took a seat on the first pew. He glanced around the cavernous sanctuary and then sat quietly.

The angel spoke again, "When this call falls upon an enamored soul, that person suddenly knows why he is in the world. God needs such souls, and they need God. Their love affair is furious. It is all madness and joy. They preach and the fire of their calling is unquenchable."[15]

"You're right. I was there once! I once felt and knew his call. But it isn't as good as you say. I can still remember how bad my early sermons were. They were unstudied and naive."

"True, but people listened to you back then, because you convinced them that you were serving a passion so mighty they dared not brush it off. They couldn't dismiss your call,

16. This must be the greatest of all sins: to tell the truth without being owned by it. James William McClendon Jr. speaks of making our biography and our theology inseparable. As long as they can be separated, we cannot be whole and preach sermons identical with ourselves. When our faith is defined by one definition and our preaching by another, we will have a hard time being believable when we do preach.

> Christian beliefs are not so many "propositions" to be catalogued or juggled like truth-functions in a computer, but are living convictions which give shape to the possibility that the only relevant critical examination of Christian beliefs may be one which begins by attending to lived lives. Theology must be at least biography. If by attending to those lives, we find ways of reforming our own theologies, making them more true, more faithful to our ancient vision, more adequate to the age now being born, then we will be justified in that arduous inquiry. Biography at its best will be theology.[16]

Theology is not what we preach. Theology is who we are, and who we are is what we preach.

17. Our sermons not only tell the world what God wants done. Our sermons tell the world who we are. Who we are is what God wants done. But all he wants done must be done relationally—within the community. The community is healthiest when the sermon is owned by those who attend it. This does not mean the sermon should not correct the community, but that even as it does, it must be free to exist for the good of the community. James Houston writes:

> There is a close connection between our need for richer human relationships and our need for intimacy with God. Each dimension (our relationship with people and with God) reinforces the other. . . . Each dimension deeply affects the other. If we find it hard to form lasting relationships with those we see around us, then we will find it very hard to relate in any depth to the God we cannot see.[17]

and you could not cast it aside. You were inflamed and captive to your passion for God.

"Lately, Sam, your preaching has been defined only by your preparation. The obsession that you once had has been bled out of you by the dull, gray leeches of programs and orthodoxy. The hot, warm blood of your commitment has been replaced by the thin plasma of telling the truth without being owned by it.[16] You used to preach to get God's work done; now you're only doing it to see if you can hold people's attention."

"But in seminary, we learned that to hold people's attention is all important."

"Important, yes, but never all important! Interest is never to be the sermon's goal. Keeping people's interest is not what you were called to do. Holding their attention is but the by-product of your calling. Your calling is to love God with so single a passion that your sermons—and more than that, your life—become a kind of fascination you cannot help and do not intend. To desire that people only become fascinated with your sermon is unworthy egotism.[17] But to be so owned by God and his desire for your life that people are drawn to you—while you never stoop to desire it—is to serve the reason you were born. The sermon is unimportant compared with this.

"Take the great preachers like Martin Luther King. Was he a great preacher because his sermons were homiletically

18. Klaus Issler says it best for me:

> There is so much more God has in mind for us than I previ-
> ously thought possible. I now live more in his grace and peace
> and love—a sense of duty motivates me less. I find myself in
> conversation with God more. As I rely more on God and pray
> more earnestly, I can discern specific answers to prayer. In a
> word, I feel more *connected* with God. Struggles and frustra-
> tions still dog my day, yet I sense less distance than before.
> With greater intensity, I appreciate how personal God is. I
> enjoy expending more effort to know God, the God who wants
> to know me.[18]

Yes, great preachers say loud and clear to their congregations, "You
are my special fruits, but even if I never say this aloud, my life will say
I am in love with God."

great? Homiletics, per se, held little interest for him. His sermons were but the by-product of the passion that he served.

"The same is true of so many megachurch pastors. They are often criticized for appearing to be show-off megamen, but the truth is they are often pastors serving God out of a single, great passion. They never set out to be famous, and when they do become well known, it is rarely because they write beautiful sermons. Indeed, their sermons often lack the homiletic excellence to which seminary textbooks point. Nonetheless, they are fascinating preachers."

"Why?"

"Because they are owned men and women. They can't be free of the love affair at the center of their souls.[18] They must hurry through life bringing pleasure, not to their Sunday hearers but to the God whose desire is their total reason to be."

"Don't they work on their sermons to make them interesting?"

"Yes. But they don't consider being interesting their calling. Sermons do not exist to fascinate. They have work to do. Truly great preachers see their sermons as the workhorse of the vision they serve. They want dreams to come true, visions to be fulfilled, lives to be changed, bent minds to be straightened. But what they want most of all is for their sermons, like everything else they own, to be owned by God.

19. I meet so many preachers with that annuity-pension-plan look. They once had a dream, but the disillusionment of the ministry stole it from them and they can't get it back. The vitality of their call is gone, and they work inflamed only by the dream of keeping their retirement annuities paid up so they can leave their dreadful work forever.

Ernest Becker wrote of Kierkegaard's man of character as a man of faith. How well this describes the office of the pastor:

> One goes through it all to arrive at faith, the faith that one's very creatureliness has some meaning to a Creator; that despite one's true insignificance, weakness, death, one's existence has meaning in some ultimate sense because it exists within an eternal and infinite scheme of things brought about and maintained to some kind of design by some creative force.[19]

20. Why the Scriptures? Because the Book we preach we know to be valid because we've already put it against our personal problems and know it works. It is the source of our worldview. Issler writes:

> Biblically minded people generally adhere to a standard threefold test of truth, of which the first test is foremost to the other two: (1) Biblical test: Is the claim in agreement with the data of Scripture (e.g., Acts 17:11)? (2) Intellectual test: Is the claim reasonable, logically consistent; does it make sense (e.g., Luke 24:11)? (3) Experiential test: Is the claim realistic, fitting within our life experience as human beings created in God's image? Does it work in life?[20]

We are servants of the Book. We preach it for three reasons:

1. It is from God.
2. It defines our view of things.
3. We know it works in life.

Our people are always to be "the people of the Book," but we are to precede them to the Book. We are the servants of the Book. We like to bring it to the people.

"Most of those preachers who turn the world upside down with their sermons start out pretty much like other preachers who achieve far less. Why? Because somewhere, many if not most preachers lose track of the dominating passion and the force of their early calling. Gradually the fire goes out and they never see the flame again.[19] And worse than this, these fizzled fireballs soon convince themselves their deadness is normal. Once they sell themselves this bill of goods, they are free to play a lot more golf."

Sam felt as though he had sat and listened long enough. "Well then, I take it the Boss has the opinion that I've left off serving my call, dropped my passions, and become a sermon writer."

"In a word, yes."

"Well, how can I correct this error?"

"There are three bases you have to cross before you can score. The first is this: quit writing sermons merely to hold interest. Second, start reading the Bible and other great devotional classics not just to find riveting sermon texts but to find the old Sam once again, that Sam who loved God and found no real reason of his own to be in this world.[20] Finally, seek God and that wonderful aura of momentary need for him. Once you commit your need to his supply on a continuing basis, your sermons will seem less important even as God seems more important. Then you will find the world turning toward a man whose sermons are more interesting because they are less important to him."

21. Why should we exalt such a need for God? We cannot preach from conviction unless we need God, for he is the source of our convictions. No wonder Os Guinness writes of the call with these words:

> Do you want to know a truth that in the momentous challenges of our modern world will be at once a quest to inspire you, an anchor to hold you fast, a rich fare to nourish you, and a relationship you will prize above all others? Listen to Jesus of Nazareth; answer his call.[21]

Sermoniel suddenly stood and smiled and said, "Ciao!"

With that, the archangel and his odd Italian farewell were gone.

His instant departure was as unnerving as it had been to encounter him in the first place. But the sting of his counsel still seemed to float in the air around Sam. He felt relieved that the angel's prescription seemed so easy. He had only to do three things to be healed. He had to abandon sermon writing as his primary reason to be. He had to find himself amid old passions he had left behind. He had to lay aside his need to be self-sufficient and find his need in God.

Then it struck him that he had the list in reverse order. First of all, he needed to need God. Then his old spiritual passions could flame once again. Finally, his frustrated attempts to write and preach interesting sermons would take care of themselves. But how was he to do this? How was he to recover this lost romance? How could he ever find a new need for God?[21]

This was the pitfall in the path of professional ministry. Everything was supplied: salary, expense accounts, hospitalization, retirement funds, library and travel allowances. It was just like God to take such good care of his children that they found they could actually do without him. Sam set aside the "perks" of his job and tried to remember that it was need— spiritual neediness—that had first caused him to come to Christ.

22. What is relevance? "Something usable in the here and now" is how many define it. But Harry Emerson Fosdick, decades ago, laid it out best for me:

> It was a great day when I began to feel sure that a sermon could be thus immediately creative and transforming. A good sermon is an engineering operation by which a chasm is bridged so that spiritual goods on one side . . . are actually transported into personal lives upon the other. . . . It need never fail to make a transforming difference in some lives.[22]

Fosdick is making no attempt to define relevance with this quote; nonetheless he does. Relevance is taking the ultimate redeeming mysteries of God and putting them to practical use in our mystery-starved world.

23. Should preaching be desperate? Should it be urgent? Isn't desperation always urgent? This may be the greatest difference between contemporary sermons and those of Jesus insofar as we are able to know how Jesus preached. Jesus seemed always to be talking of things that were urgent and must be taken care of now.

How modern sermons need to start and end with such desperation. Alister McGrath reminds us of Barth's comment on Jesus' urgency:

> When Holy Scripture speaks of God, it does not permit us to let our attention or thoughts wander at random. . . . When Holy Scripture speaks of God, it concentrates our attention and thoughts upon one single point and what is to be known at that point. . . . If we ask further concerning the one point upon which, according to Scripture, our attention and thoughts should and must be concentrated, then from first to last the Bible directs us to the name of Jesus Christ.[23]

If modern sermons could refine this important and lost urgency, the resulting passion would overfill our churches.

Sam found he had to think on another level to remember the definition of his neediness. His sermons had become pretty here and now. *Relevant* was the big word in preaching. Relevant meant that preaching had to dispense truth that worked in the here and now. But the really important truths could never be captive to the here and now. What good was the here and now if it didn't touch base with things enduring and eternal?[22]

In fact, eternity was so much larger than the here and now that no sermon which did not concern itself with things eternal stood little chance of ever being relevant. Sam had a lot of soul-searching to do. Were there such places as heaven and hell? Was this life really the porch of the grand house we call eternity? Could Sam live without Jesus? Would he want to? Was life as desperate as Jesus indicated when he said, "There is a broad road that leads to destruction and many there are who go down that road, because straight is the road and narrow is the way that leads to life and few there be who find it"? Was the world that desperate? If it was really in the kind of trouble Jesus talked about, Sam felt that he had grown increasingly easy with the desperation of all those who never came to know Christ.[23]

Sam hated thinking these dour thoughts, and yet he realized that if there was anything to these things, most pulpits he knew about were missing the point by a mile. Sam had himself. Preaching was a calling that God gave to those he called,

24. The desperation of the sermon was born with a missionary *raison d'être*. The sermon was not given to the church to snuggle into the liturgy to make worship interesting. The sermon was given a task—an urgent task. It was the watchman on the wall.

Years ago I wrote this in the book *Spirit, Word, and Story:*

> Urgency takes no time for irrelevancies. John the Baptist would not even answer the simple question, "What is your name?" In essence, he said, "My name ... my name? What matters my name? I am a crying voice—flee from the fire!" (see John 1:22–23). Perhaps the long introductions of guest preachers today points out the change between first-century urgency and the casual propriety of sermons today. Some contemporary sermons are little more than moral speeches that tip their homiletical hats to God. The fearsome trumpets of fiery desperation have at last only settled into our chatty liturgy.[24]

25. Great sermons move around the cute or even the speculative. Great sermons answer real issues, not just interesting discussions.

> There is only one question of real importance: "Is this sermon for me right now?" Their ignorance of Scripture reveals their need. David H. C. Read said, "I learned, when a university chaplain, that the student who asked where Cain got his wife could really be wanting to know whether he should sleep with his girlfriend."[25]

and it was a burden heavy to be borne. Yet Sam felt that he and most of the preachers who were his colleagues and friends had grown casual in their responsibility to clue the world in. Most preachers he knew, like himself, were working at merely holding people's attention. In fact, it seemed to him that many homiletics books were too consumed with this. Preachers who could do this were always popular, but no matter the preacher! There was a sin in dismissing the real duty of preaching to glory in the perks of popularity and acceptance. The real work of world-changing had completely slipped their homiletic focus.

Indeed, Christianity was in the business of urgency. The word *Jesus* meant "God saves," and *saved* was the word that the New Testament so often applied to the human predicament.[24] Saved was a desperate word, and sermons were desperate ways of dealing with the desperation. Once again, Sam felt ashamed. To try to be interesting or clever was a kind of sermonic cheap shot when the world was so much in need of redemption.

Further, he began to see why he and so many preachers he knew were so bored with their jobs. Their preaching was trivial. Boredom had always been the bedfellow of triviality. Cute lay at one end of trivial interest. Silly at the other. What never bored were brokenness, redemption, and soul renovation.[25]

If heaven and hell were real and eternal, then the sermon should exist as a call, an existential cry of hope. Sermons

26. Howard Macy makes it quite clear that the megachurch addiction to user-friendly methodology may be too congenial to venture into the world of severe honesty. The sermon was not intended to be a smiley mask over the face of a requiring God. Macy puts it this way:

> From the Cathedral of the Perpetual Smile to First Happy Baptist, there are plenty of people who would mistakenly have us believe that the life of faith is basically one long joyride. To sustain this illusion and the quest for the Holy Grin, they transform the church program into a religious amusement park hawking a thrill-a-minute, fun-filled experience, complete with emotional roller coasters, religious variety shows, verbal trick mirrors, and more. Such teaching is a half-truth at best, a shoddy imitation of authentic joy in faith.[26]

27. We all need to stand before the text and face the almightiness of Christ's word. We must then face the mirror and stare at our humanness with all the things that might present themselves as a barrier to God's Word. As we stand there, we depend upon God's view of us to instruct us. Crenshaw puts it this way:

> Indeed, the texts for today stand convicted by a higher morality, one to which Abraham of old appealed in the stinging question "Shall not the Judge of all the earth act in a right and just manner?" Still, I join hands with the authors of the texts in pleading guilty before a higher tribunal.[27]

sinned by entertaining when they ought to shout out warnings. It was after a season of such pointless sermons that the nursery rhyme was born:

> The rector is late, he's forgotten the date,
> So what will the faithful do now, poor things!
> They'll sit in the pew with nothing to do,
> And sing a collection of hymns, poor things!

Sam realized that most churches were bewildered by preachers who devoted themselves to long talks on nonessential subjects. The world was more desperate than it knew.[26] Sam was more desperate than he knew. He was called to be a kind of watchman on the wall, a sermonizing sentry ordering the church to advance into an uncharted eternity.

People who felt important things intently attracted attention and wonder. Hence the likely apocryphal statement of D. L. Moody: "Get on fire for Jesus and the world will come to watch you burn." Sam, however, did not want to trump up some hyperdesperate mood out of which he might thunder forth melodrama. Needing God was not something you laid siege to, like overcoming inferiority. The key was to take your humanity to God and confess that poor protoplasm was the most we could surrender. Nor would Sam trump up a preacher's tone so he could appear to be sincere, even when he didn't mean it. No, Sam would give himself to the business of transformation.[27]

28. How do we make sermons important? The real crux, perhaps the only crucial question, is, "Does this sermon say what God wants said?" If it does so, then it is important.

John Stott equates the issue of important preaching to relevance:

> We should be praying that God will raise up a new generation of Christian communicators who are determined to bridge the chasm; who struggle to relate God's unchanging Word to our ever-changing world; who refuse to sacrifice truth to relevance or relevance to truth; but who resolve instead in equal measure to be faithful to Scripture and pertinent to today.[28]

29. Calvin Miller, *A Covenant for All Seasons.*[29]

30. The text is the thing! Without it the sermon gets too far afield from what God says, and we have only the pitiful word of man. Allan Bloom said of books in general:

> Without the great revelations, epics and philosophies as part of our natural vision, there is nothing to see out there, and eventually little left inside. The Bible is not the only means to furnish a mind, but without a book of similar gravity, read with the gravity of the potential believer, it will remain unfurnished.[30]

Without the Bible there is no sermon. The Bible is the book which gives root to the sermon. The sermon is a sermon because it's about the Bible. Otherwise it is just a speech.

The time had come for a new dependency on Christ, and Sam was ready to commit himself. He once again fell on his knees in the darkened chapel and said, half-aloud in the darkness, "God, help me not to preach better. Just help me to be better. Do nothing for my reputation. Only bring me to the place where I see what needs to be done, and make me alive for the doing of it. Don't make my sermons interesting; make them important. Let them seek no critiques as to their eloquence or boredom. Only let them be a cry on your behalf for all you want done in the world."[28]

Sam rose from his knees. He knew that one cannot make a once-for-all commitment to cover every future slippage. Commitments were to be made at every moment. Hath not the poet said, "Old promises must pledge themselves each day / Or unrenewed pass quietly away"?[29] Still, his daily need for God must allow each moment to make him the dependent pastor he needed to be. So when he rose from prayer, there was still much to be done.

He faced his sermon preparation for the next morning. But now that he had voiced his new commitment to caring about God, he found that he was committed to needing God. Nothing dampened this need. Finally, he arrived at the hard part of his soon-to-be-delivered sermon. He was ready to move his sermon from being interesting to necessary. But how?

He had to ask himself one really hard question. Was the text he had already picked set to do the work of God?[30] What

31. What is the Bible if not a personal guide to who God is and what he wants done? So along with picking the text, the task of the preacher is to live in that Scripture until he knows what God wants done. Then let the preacher live in that text a little longer till he or she has the courage to write a sermon which does it. Eugene Lowry writes:

> The kind of preaching Rose calls *transformational* is what some others have called the new homiletic. Terms most often associated with this kind of preaching are *event* and *encounter* (a somewhat different encounter from that imaged in kerygmatic style). The "power of performative language to shape human consciousness" (or to evoke a new orientation) is central to some versions of this kind of preaching.[31]

If the sermon doesn't get done what God wants done, it is not a sermon. Sermons by definition state the agenda of God in a world which doesn't know that agenda or care about it.

32. Sermons must always answer the question of who God is and what he expects. Brown Taylor said this in her Yale lectures:

> I listened to an Easter sermon once in which the preacher stood up in front of a church full of people hungry for good news and told us Easter bunny jokes, one after another. He never met our eyes. He looked up at the light fixtures as he delivered his punch lines, never noticing how we laughed less each time. Finally he said something about how Easter was God's joke on death and we should all laugh more. Then he said *Amen* and sat down. I have never in my life wished so badly for pulpit police. I wanted someone with a badge to go up and arrest that guy, slap some handcuffs on him, and lead him away.[32]

Why did she wish this? Because she had been to church, listened to a sermon, and left the sermon knowing less about the agenda of God in the world than when she went.

was it that God wanted done? Who was he called to be? He turned the idea over in his head again and again and finally admitted that he was about to fall short.

Now was the moment.

This was the time.

What did God want done, and how was Sam to get it done by preaching?[31]

His text for the morning was Joshua 24:15: "As for me and my house, we will serve the Lord." Sam had planned to preach on how to have an ideal home life, so that those who didn't have it would somehow get it and they would all be happier families. Suddenly he could see that for families to be happy wasn't enough. Families needed to know why they were all living in the same house at the same time. What do children and mothers and fathers owe God that defines why they are all living in the same part of the world?[32]

The next morning, the sermon flew from a man who had just been given sight to a congregation all too ready to receive it. Sam found that in saying what God wanted said, the potential force of people's acceptance or criticism lost its control over him. Yet they listened—and harder than they ever had—but their listening was no longer Sam's goal.

When the sermon was over and all the guests had been greeted, Sam went back to the vestry to take off his pulpit robe. He was surprised to find Emma Johnson, his faithful longtime critic, waiting at the door of his study.

33. Preaching—Bible preaching—can do more than we think it can do. Sometimes we preachers forget this. We build sermons on the Bible and nothing seems to happen to the audience. What happens to the preacher is that he or she begins to lower the expectation of the sermon. Sermons can do more than we preachers generally think they can when we preach them. Willhite says:

> This is where relevant, biblical preaching begins, continues, and ends; from the specifics of and making exegetical decisions or "I need an illustration," all the way through to praying that my heart will be right before God as I preach and that people will come prepared to hear and do the Word of God. There is absolutely no substitute for prayer and the power of the Holy Spirit in preaching.[33]

34. Preaching can do much, but often it only performs to the level of the preacher's expectation. It can do little more than the preacher dreams for it. The preacher must select a text which best suits the agenda of God for the sermon. Then he must outline the task of the sermon for the text. Then some plan for the text must be established so the preacher will know how to achieve the task. Only then will the sermon stay informal as it is preached. Only then will the preacher know how to begin and end the sermon. Hugh Litchfield writes:

> After reading and listening to hundreds, yea thousands, of sermons, I am convinced that their greatest weakness is a lack of focus. They often go everywhere, leading to confusion and bewilderment. A pastor, having listened to such a rambling sermon, made the judgment, "When he got up to preach, he didn't know where he was going and when he sat down, he didn't know where he'd been."[34]

"Sam, you remember my nephew Charlie, don't you?"

"Hi Charlie!" said Sam. He studied the teenaged youth before him. He was a handsome boy with deep-set eyes and studied features.

"Well, Sam, Charlie was moved by your sermon. Now he thinks he wants to be a preacher. It would absolutely ruin his career in law.[33] His dad would have none of that, and so I wanted to give you the chance to talk him out of it." Emma Johnson was being especially brusque, but Sam was in no mood to be bullied.

"Why do you think you want to be a preacher, Charlie?" asked Sam.

"I can see that nothing else matters but God, and it's all I really want for my life."

"When did you come to this conclusion, Charlie?" Sam put his arm around the shoulder of the young man.

"Well, I've been thinking about it for a long time, but it wasn't till I heard your sermon this morning that I became really convinced."

"Who convinced you?"

"Well, it must have been the Lord. You see, sir, your sermon convinced me that nothing really matters but what God wants with our lives. Your sermon changed my desire to have what I thought I wanted for what I now see that God wants. Do you think preaching can do that?"[34]

Sam hugged the boy.

35. Nobody knows why some ordinary moment of some ordinary sermon is the very place God chooses to get his work done. It is all part of the mystery of God. Good preaching does not attempt to clear up this mystery. It lets the mystery live, for we all know that when there is no mystery, God is not present. Brown Taylor writes:

> If God is more present in silence than in words, if our best works cannot aspire to more than pointing toward the God who is beyond them, then what are we to make of the Incarnate Word? Jesus could have come to us as the Incarnate Silence, after all, or as the Incarnate Mystery.[35]

Mrs. Johnson was clearly agitated.

"It could be, Emma," said Sam, "that God has called this boy to preach the gospel."

"It could be, pastor, that you got him so worked up he *thinks* he's called to preach the gospel. You called him; you *uncall* him, right now before I take him home and his parents raise the roof."

"Auntie Em," said Charlie, "it's no use. Pastor Sam didn't call me and he can't uncall me. Things like this happen during sermons and nobody but God knows why."[35]

Emma and Charlie were soon gone, but Charlie's words wouldn't leave Sam's mind. Sam was sure of one thing, the sermon that Sunday morning had work to do and it had done it. But Charlie's "call to preach" was only one of the things that happened. The other was that Sam had been healed by his own preaching. He had no idea whether the sermon was good or bad. That was hardly the point. The sermon had been possessed by a great God who had an agenda with a needy preacher and at least one other young man. Charlie—plain ole Charlie—had met God at the low altar of a needy sermon drawn from the life of a needy preacher.

"God," Sam prayed, "I can hardly wait till next week."

On the way out of his office to his car, Sam passed by the front of the pulpit. There he saw a huge white feather lying under the first pew just off the center aisle.

36. Giving God our need and waiting on his supply tells us why we're in the world, but it tells us more than that: great preaching accentuates our call. We belong to Jesus. So does the Bible; so do our listeners. We should enter the sermon remembering that God is entering with us ready to take us and our words and use them for his glory. Abraham Kuyper said of all of life:

> There is not one square inch of the entire creation about which Jesus Christ does not cry out, "This is mine! This belongs to me!"[36]

This is true of the godly preacher and all that is preached.

"Shedding, Sermoniel?" he asked, turning the feather over in his hand. "I don't know if you can hear me, but I just remembered why I'm in the world."

He carried the feather out into the sunlight. He walked to his car and opened the door.

"Lord," he said, "I give you my need. I wait on your supply."[36]

Sam had turned a corner. He had gone back to his future. He had found the Sam he had foolishly mislaid. Nothing mattered now but his need.

1. How often the sense of failure occupies the preacher. We often have the feeling that we're not doing enough. So often the preacher's Monday morning feelings of failure have to do with one thing: my sermons and their preaching are not good enough to keep me from a low opinion of myself. John Killinger rightly surmises that feelings of failure are so debilitating:

> Now we arrive at the real test of the preacher's dedication to the task of preaching—whether he or she is willing to pay for the actual shaping of the sermon. It is one thing to entertain glorious dreams of what one could do. But it is quite another thing to be willing to work at it, to carry it in one's thoughts day and night, to tinker with outlines or sermon plans until they are just right, to sweat over the wording till it is at once vivid and precise, and finally to get it all inside one's head for preaching, the way one gets a firm hold on any important word to be said to people who really matter.[37]

TWO

THE COMPULSIVE FOLLY

It takes more than a single battle to lay siege to a settled empire. Sermoniel's white feather lay oddly on Sam's desk reminding him of his long-ago night with the Angel of Homiletics and the Sunday fire which followed. But the fires in his soul were burning low. It came to pass that in the fullness of time, Sam's new passion for preaching was blunted once again by a sense of failure. He knew what the spirit of the sermon should be, but the form its words should take often eluded him. His new discontent should not have surprised him. Preaching is neither a career nor a finished art. It changes and retreats, advances and lives. Once again he found Monday mornings intolerable. The fire of why he preached had been doused by the ice water of homiletic method—how it should be done. "Lord, I'm so tired of preaching . . . so tired of saying the same things to these same people every week."

Pastor Sam was discouraged.[1] He once again felt that odd sameness that came to him on Monday mornings.

2. Writing a ten-minute quickie is not a good way to arrive at life-changing preaching. The sermon that counts grows slowly through the agony and ecstasy of planning, prayer, and rehearsal. Killinger writes:

> Few preachers possess the brilliance or facility of James Pike, the famous and controversial bishop of California, who had a disturbingly casual approach to preaching. Pike said he gave some thought to sermon material on Saturday night, consulted a few commentaries, and formed a "kind of outline" in his mind. He reflected on the outline before going to bed and again in the morning. Then he went into the pulpit and preached, usually without any notes at all. . . . Great preachers, however, seldom agree with Pike's assessment. Most of them have worked assiduously at their sermons, the way great novelists work at their novels or great poets work at their poetry. Sangster chose his sermon themes at least ten days in advance and then worked at the sermons every day until they were preached. George A. Buttrick spent a minimum of twenty-five to thirty hours on each sermon he was to deliver—in most cases, more than an hour per minute for the finished product. Paul Scherer sometimes devoted forty hours to a single sermon.
>
> Who was it, Paderewski, who once played for Queen Victoria? When he had finished the Queen said, "Mr. Paderewski, you are a genius!" "That may be, madam," replied Paderewski, "but years before I was a genius, I was a drudge."[38]

Neither Pike's theology nor his sermon preparation are to be esteemed. The preacher's theology must come from Scripture; so must the cause and the form of the sermon.

3. What should be the language of the sermon? Needless to say it must be the common language of the auditors. Sam is probably in the wrong for deliberately antagonizing his members with his choice of words. The point is too minor to need to win. It is better to use new ways of expressing the old gospel but not to use terms that antagonize. Charles Campbell, referring to Fred Craddock, writes:

> We ought to lay aside old terms and phrases, including the biblical idiom itself. [Craddock] argues that the church needs a retirement program for old words, which simply do not work anymore. Craddock does not discuss with any care how we go

"Same, Lord, do you hear me? Same, same, same. I'm praying the same prayer after I preach the same sermon to the same crowd the same way every same week. And this is the most ludicrous of all, the grand jest to end all jests: even my name, Sam, is just the word *same* with the *e* left off.

"Lord, why is it that some people get called to work for Exxon with loads of profit-sharing, stock options, and fringe benefits, and I get called to the futile work of preaching? And me an evangelical! I have to preach twice a week. Why couldn't you have at least called me to preach in a more liturgical church? Nobody listens to their sermons either, but they only have to do it once a week. Besides, they use so much time in the liturgy of their worship services, they can get by on ten-minute quickies all the way to retirement."[2]

After he stopped praying, Sam did the same two things he did every Monday morning: first, he picked up *Golf Digest*. Then he clamped his eyes shut and asked God to please let him wake up in Bermuda.

It happened every Monday morning; he had PMS—post-melancholy sermonitis.

Yes, he thought, *I've been called to preach! And while I keep looking for a bigger church that feels called to listen, this is my lot in life. My karma, dharma, my kismet.* He remembered even as he thought of the terms how Mrs. Johnson recently had rebuked him for using Eastern religious words in his sermon.[3] Just the memory of that caused him to stiffen his spine and shout to

about finding a new language, other than suggesting implicitly that it must somehow express and evoke the same experience once expressed in the old one.[39]

4. It may seem ludicrous for the preacher to buttress his conversation with a Scripture passage, and yet preachers ought to get used to making every point of the sermon as scriptural as they can. It gives our every sentence authority. William Bouknight also says, tongue in cheek:

> The following advertisement was posted in a Christian bookstore:
>
> > The Word of God—truth divine.
> > Leather bound, only 7.99.
> > It scares the devil when he sees
> > Bibles sold as cheap as these.
>
> Most American mainline Protestants believe that the entire Bible was inspired by God.[40]

The Word exists to furnish not just the sermon. It exists to occupy the hearts of both the preacher and the parishioner.

5. My point in making the angel a part of Sam's preparation is simply to remind us that preachers write and deliver great sermons with one foot in the supernatural realm and one in the present world. Theodore Roszak once likened the preacher to a shaman or witch doctor. He remarked that the shaman, in a primitive community, is one through whose life otherworldly forces are seen to be at work. Great preaching comes in power from the world of the Spirit to touch and change the world at hand.

the lonely walls of his study, "Karma, dharma, kismet! Take that, Sister Johnson!" and then added, "You fat, fat cow of Bashan." Then he offered the citation, "That's Amos 4:1, Emma Johnson, you old hen."[4] He suddenly felt ashamed for being so severe. Still, he wished *hen* were in the book of Amos too so he could tell her what he really thought. He really didn't know which he disliked more: preaching or Emma Johnson. All he knew was that neither of them gave him great joy on Monday mornings when he was a quivering clot of discouragement.

"Discouraged?" asked a voice from the corner of the room.

Sam peered into the shadows. His hair stood on the back of his neck. An odd chill followed by a flush of fever destroyed his reverie. It was Sermoniel, the Angel of Homiletics! He hadn't seen Sermoniel since their first encounter, but he had often felt he was lurking around the dark corridors of Sam's lonely moments. His sudden appearance left Sam more startled than terrified.[5]

Then Sermoniel spoke. "Fear not! For behold . . . Now where have I heard that before?"

"Luke 2:10," offered Sam. "Really, there's no need to tell me to 'fear not!' You need to know that I'm very hard to frighten. I've been Mrs. Johnson's pastor for seven years, seven lean years—thin as the kine of Egypt that have now devoured the fat cows of all my seminary confidence."

6. Preaching has been the glory of the church. There is much argument over whether it still is or will long remain so. In spite of the current flurry of interest in preaching, all the signs for its future are not all that gratifying. Charles Campbell writes:

> Over the past twenty-five years homiletics has enjoyed growing vitality. And today the field seems as strong as ever. New preaching books are published almost daily. Homiletical conferences, journals, and resources multiply. Doctoral programs turn out specialized professors who are in demand in the seminaries. New theories and forms of preaching abound at every turn. These are unquestionably exciting days for homiletics.
>
> Beneath the surface, however, signs of trouble can be discerned. The new preaching theories and resources do not appear to have brought new life to the church.[41]

7. The question is what's happened to preaching. Where went its great reputation and its history, which in some ways was the key thread in the fabric of the West?

While homiletics is popular, Campbell writes,

> mainline churches have been in decline. The multiplication of preaching theories has taken place alongside a growing concern, even despair, about the life and future of the church. Recent homiletical developments seem to have accomplished little more than to rearrange the proverbial deck chairs on the Titanic.[42]

8. It is not true that people are liking sermons less. But it is true that the requirements of the current generation are more stringent than of previous generations. Warren Wiersbe suggests that the kind of sermons people hear is getting radically different than those the previous generation preferred:

> I think sermons are getting shorter. Bob Cook used to tell us in Youth for Christ that a sermon does not have to be eternal to be immortal. Sermons are getting shorter, preaching is getting more personal, and the preacher has to be more open and more transparent. The day is over when people simply accept the authority of the text; they also need to be assured of the authority of the preacher. When I started my ministry over

"I come to earth to help out preachers only after they quit reading Fred Craddock and start reading *Golf Digest*. You know you were given a glorious calling, preaching. It's got a pretty good history. Savonarola preached; John Chrysostom too. Richard Baxter preached. Preaching is glory![6] Jesus did it. The apostle Paul, John Calvin, and Martin Luther too."

Sam adjusted himself in his chair. "Well don't get cocky, Sermoniel. Benny Hinn and Robert Tilton also do it."

"Nonetheless," said Sermoniel, "preaching has always been the glory of the church."

"Well, it's not working out so good anymore."

"If you think that, you need to go back and read Savonarola's sermon at the stake. Now that was real preaching, the kind of preaching that will make you hang your ordination certificate back up and try again."

"Savonarola was a little martyr. I've got Mrs. Johnson. I live on the stake week after week."

"Hey, Sam, cheer up! Preaching is the glory of the church.[7] Did you know that the word *preaching* or some derivative of it is used 162 times in the Bible and fifty of those times in the New Testament? The subject comes up twelve times in First Corinthians alone."

"Fascinating! But my congregation doesn't like preaching very much.[8] I'm into being popular for a while. Is there anything in the Bible on the NFL?"

forty years ago, a preacher would not tell publicly about some dumb thing he did last week, but now many preachers do it. I think preaching is changing for the better, if what I read is what people are hearing. I think there are some fine young preachers coming along. I won't name them but I am grateful for what God is doing in and through them. They're better trained than I was when I got started and they have better tools.[43]

9. First Corinthians 1:18, 21–24 is the passage upon which this story is based—hence the title "The Compulsive Folly." Paul reminds us that the sermon is a kind of foolishness that redeems. Preaching can be an oddly done business, and yet it has been the chief method of advance for the kingdom of God. Why preaching? Because it is from the Bible, writes Killinger, and

> the Bible is about the community but it is also about God. It is about God's struggling with the community through the years, shaping it in an act of creation far more risky and difficult than the creation of the world itself.

The sermon is important critical and imperative folly, for the sermon is talking about God,

> and talking about God is more important than anything else we can do for people. Where else in the world will they hear about God? The preacher who has abandoned talking about God has abandoned our *raison d'etre,* our calling to be proclaimers.[44]

10. The compulsive sense of our calling in a sense operates on two levels. First there is that primary sense of calling that we receive when first we enter the ministry. We return to that sense of calling again and again. It is that first big emphasis that we go back to repeatedly and that anchors our profession to a God-connectedness for life. But there is also a second more momentary sense of calling. That sense travels with us during every waking moment to remind us that what we see and experience, that everything we touch, is useful for our preaching. Martin Luther said:

> Only look at your tools, your needles, your thimble, your beer barrel, your articles of trade, your scales, your measures, and

"Sam, you need to open your Bible to 1 Corinthians 1:18, 21–24 and then finish up with 1 Corinthians 9:14–16."

Sam paused as though he would refuse, then thought better of it and flipped through a worn thumb index. "Okay. Here it is." Sam began to read.

"Well, read it."

"Aloud?"

"Yes, man, aloud; that's how sermon texts should be read—aloud."

Sam rolled his eyes. He didn't like bossy angels, but he thought it better to obey than argue. He stiffened his spine and began reading. "'For the message of the cross is foolishness to those who are perishing, but to us who are being saved it is the power of God. . . . For since in the wisdom of God the world through its wisdom did not know him, God was pleased through the foolishness of what was preached to save those who believe. Jews demand miraculous signs and Greeks look for wisdom, but we preach Christ crucified: a stumbling block to the Jews and foolishness to Gentiles.'"[9]

After some additional thumbing through the tissue pages, Sam read again.

"'Yet when I preach the gospel, I cannot boast, for I am compelled to preach. Woe to me if I do not preach the gospel!'"[10]

"You see, Sam, Paul said preaching the gospel is glorious work! Do you happen to have copies of your three most recent sermons?"

69

you will find this saying written on them. You will not be able to look anywhere, where it does not strike your eyes. None of the things with which you deal daily are too trifling to tell you this incessantly, if you are but willing to hear it; and there is no lack of such preaching, for you have as many preachers as there are transactions, commodities, tools and other implements in your house and estate, and they shout this to your face: "My dear, use me toward your neighbor, as you would want him to act toward you with that which is his."[45]

Preachers walk past the best illustrations and metaphors. But they can never include them in a sermon if they never see them.

11. Many preachers see exposition as a matter of verse-by-verse illumination. Let me assure the preacher who preaches this way that I am not against this method. What I am against is boredom. So often preachers who preach this way are not very interesting, but for the few who are, I say "bravo!" Besides being boring, verse-by-verse preaching often fails to correlate the widely separate parts of the Bible, so the listeners are focused so intently on a single word or phrase that they ignore the rest of the truth in the Scriptures.

But the equal and opposite charge can be brought against the Scripture generalist. Those who preach on a verse here and there, hit and miss, often fail to get specific enough at any point that the Bible ever speaks in an in-depth way. It is this unfortunate tendency that John MacArthur finds so distasteful:

If I received five letters in the mail one day, it would make no sense to read a sentence or two out of one, skip two, read a few sentences out of another, and go on to the next one and read a few out of that, and on and on. If I really want to comprehend the letter—what is going on, the tone, the spirit, the attitude, and the purpose—I must start from the beginning and go on to the end of each one. If that is true of personal correspondence, then how much more is it so of divine revelation.[46]

12. Naming the sermon is critical. Until a sermon is named, it struggles to find a place in our memories. Our thoughts about how we want to say something remain nebulous till we name them. Speaking of a bad call that led to a baseball brouhaha, umpire Satchel Paige cried, "It ain't nothin' till I call it." In a real sense, a sermon cannot amount to much if we refuse to name it. I wrote in *Marketplace Preaching:*

Dutifully, Sam handed him copies of his last three sermons. "They're all from Romans 13," said Sam.[11]

"All three of them? Isn't that a little overkill?"

Sam bristled. "I've been preaching through a thirty-two-sermon series titled 'First-Israel, Second-Israel, and the Nature of the Holy Covenants in Transition.'"[12]

"Sounds fascinating, but Sam, thirty-two sermons . . . and just look at these three on Romans 13," Sermoniel said. "The first one is called 'Designing Doctrine to Deal with the Devil,' the second is 'Destiny, Debt, and the Divine Deliverer,' and the last is 'Debauchery, Dissension, and Demonic Delusion.' Furthermore, look, Sam, there's not a single story or illustration in any one of the three."

"I'm passionate about God. I don't waste time telling people stories."

"Well, are people flocking to hear you? Is your church growing?"

"Actually, the crowd is getting so thin that they can all gather around my digital projector and warm their hands on cold Sunday mornings. To be honest, our church has grown from 220 to ninety-three in a single year. But I don't get too discouraged. The Word of God said it would be this way, you know. We're now in the seventh part of the seventh dispensation. You know, the age of the great apostasy. The falling away from the truth that will characterize the end days. I've got a

On Monday at least a working title should be agreed upon. This will enable the pastor to do what Ian Pitt-Watson suggests in his excellent book—that a sermon should grow within us as a baby grows inside her mother. . . . Whether at our desk or not, we will find gladsome content sticking like Velcro to our growing theme.[47]

13. In picturing how discriminating listeners attend to a sermon, Warren Wiersbe has this to say about alliterative outlines. He pictures Grandma Thatcher, who says concerning her pastor's alliterative preaching style:

"Last week it was all S's. Today it's all CP's."

She settled back in the pew, turned the preacher off, and began meditating on the psalm read earlier that morning before George had gotten up to menace her day.[48]

14. It is important in communication to depend on uninterrupted eye contact to communicate. The most powerful kind of communication is eye to eye. To refer to a screen or even a printed outline during the message gives the hearers a reason to look away from the speaker's eyes. At that very moment, something wonderful is lost: the power of seeing "eye to eye." I wrote in *Spirit, Word, and Story*:

Many preachers look over the heads of their listeners in a kind of fake eye contact that really shuts out the audience. One such preacher to whom I listened confided afterward that he found it much easier to "look just over their heads than to look into their eyes." Nonetheless it was clear to all present that he was having a conversation with the back wall and not with them. He would never have held a personal conversation in such a way. Why then would he elect to preach in such a cold and affected manner? Eye must meet eye and heart must meet heart, for real emotional encounter to occur.[49]

seventeen-slide sermon on that too. It's called 'The Dissipation of Devotion in the Dreadful Day of Doom.'"

"Sam, do all your sermons have these remote alliterative titles?"[13]

"What do you mean 'remote alliteration'? Alliteration is my gift of the Spirit." Sam was all aglow now. "I'm good at it too; just look at the subpoints of this sermon called 'Debauchery, Dissension, and Demonic Delusion'; they're all alliterative."

Sermoniel said, "Hmm ... I see what you mean. Point 1, 'Decency Disregarded Is Debauchery.' Point 2, 'Dogma Disregarded Is Dissension.' And Point 3, 'Deception Deferred Is Delusion.'"

Sam was beaming now. "You oughta see my slides; they're breathtaking. I color all those *d*'s red. Then I put little flames around the bottom of them. They look terrifyingly premillenial in PowerPoint."[14]

"Sam, no wonder people are going to sleep during your sermons. This stuff is dry as dust. Dust ... you know dust? It's that stuff that is dry, dirty, desperate, and despicable."

"All the people said this was a great sermon on Romans 13!"

"All?"

"All who came. Except for Sister Johnson. She always reminds me that my sermons meant so much to her late husband after he lost his mind. She does agree with me on apostasy and the last days, but she thinks that it's my sermons

15. Remember, we shouldn't use a narrative preaching style just to hold interest. If this temptation is served too much, the sermon may be interesting but not very vital in terms of teaching the audience the heart of Scripture. David Larsen sounds a wise word here:

> Homeliticians and theologians of the left, having essentially surrendered the Bible to modernity, are scrambling frenetically to snatch something of significance from Scripture to fill the yawning abyss of emptiness. Thus has come the stampede toward preaching narrative and doing theology narratively.[50]

16. Precept preaching lends itself to alliterative outlines and vice versa. But taking notes on a sermon is not the point of preaching. Changed lives is the point of preaching. The words of Scripture are to point to the Word of Scripture, even to Jesus. Precepts given for the sake of alliteration and note-taking may fill a notebook and pass through the auditor on to the pages of the auditor's notebook without changing the note-taker's life or necessarily causing him or her to think of Jesus. Note-taking always points to the precepts of a sermon rather than to the narrative aspects of a sermon. Why? As I wrote in *Spirit, Word, and Story*:

> We rarely take notes during stories. Notes are the inky tracks of precept preaching. Pencils and pads have a way of keeping hands so busy that minds do not notice they are sleepy. In churches where note taking is essential to self-esteem, the entire congregation may need to ask, "Without my pencil and pad, could I stand to listen one hour to him?"[51]

17. Is 90 percent of the Bible narrative? This statement is a tad hyperbolic. The Bible is a storybook, but we mustn't minimize preaching in either the direction of being largely story or largely precept. Charles Swindoll won my esteem years ago for achieving just the proper balance between story and precept. I have long been his fan because I conceive the best sermons to be a stacking of precepts and stories in which the precept is allowed to state the truth and story is allowed to make it fascinating. Precepts feed, but the story creates the appetite for wanting to gorge ourselves on the important epistemological truths of the Bible. Says Swindoll:

that are single-handedly bringing on this great turning away from the faith."[15]

"It's probably an overstatement," said Sermoniel, "but take this thirteenth chapter of Romans. Do you realize that this is the famous *tole-lege* passage that Augustine read and was converted? Have you thought about just telling your people the story of his salvation? It wouldn't even take much preparation to tell; it's all right in the *Confessions*. But never forget one other thing that Augustine said. He actually referred to the sermon as the *narratio*, or the story. Imagine that, Augustine actually referred to the whole sermon as the *narratio*. Now Sam, there isn't an ounce of *narratio* in five pounds of your alliteration."[16]

"I told you, I don't tell my people stories."

"Well, you know G. Hinton Davies said that the Bible is 90 percent narrative and only 10 percent precept.[17] Why don't you try preaching a narrative next Sunday and see what might happen? Maybe you could simply tell them the story of your call to preach."

Suddenly Sermoniel faded and was gone.

Sam sighed and stared at the vacant place Sermoniel had lately occupied. Gradually his wandering mind settled into a reflective state. Maybe God had sent this homiletic seraph to help him get his ministry going in a new direction. Sam picked up his ballpoint pen and scratched his title at the top of the page: "'The Compulsive Folly' by Sam." He began to write.

Truth, made clear through the use of just the right illustration, anecdote, story or quotation, is applied more quickly and remembered much longer.[52]

18. Old habits are hard to break. Nothing is harder than seeing a sermonic weakness and setting out to change it. The preacher must ever confront this weakness, rather like an actor contemplates a new role on the stage. Actors spend hours of rehearsal just to capture a mannerism or an accent used in the role they have been assigned to portray. Preachers too must ever be rehearsing, taking up new roles, and doing daring new things before their audience. In every sermon, preachers should be bringing something new to their audience. Such continual newness will require a flexibility of homiletic style that grabs for audience interest. Marsh Cassady had this to say about creativity:

> It is catching and holding fast a fleeting moment of truth in a painting, a piece of clay, or a poem. It is discovering a new interpretation or taking something that already exists and changing it in an unpredictable way.[53]

Preaching—particularly precept preaching—will become quite predictable, unless the preacher intentionally takes arms against predictability. But to do this the preacher must be willing to act so as to be uncomfortable with the changes he demands of himself. As we force ourselves into communication styles with which we are not comfortable, we take a stand against a killing sameness in the pulpit.

19. It is amazing how important it is to keep in touch with our calling. The preacher who has a concrete experience of the call will go back to that call again and again as an important, if mystical, credential for his or her sermonizing. Sometimes we must preach when we are discouraged. At those moments it is important—as Sam puts it—to remember how we got into preaching in the first place. W. E. Sangster said:

> Called to preach! That is the basic thing at last. Let a man be sure of that, and keep his certitude by obedience, and he will have the answer to all the doubts that dog the steps of a preacher regarding his vocation. . . . Only a divine commission can justify it. Lacking that is a gross impertinence. No humble

"When I was seventeen years old and a senior in high school, I was going through a period of spiritual dryness. But God came to me and said, 'Sam, your problem is that you are depleted, discouraged, disappointed, and debilitated.'"[18] As he wrote this alliterative outline down, a huge ballpoint pen came down out of the ceiling of his study, marked through the alliterative list, and wrote, "Get real and try again!" Sam knew it was Sermoniel. He had always prayed for God's help in writing his sermons, but this was a little more than he felt comfortable with.

He thought for a moment or two.

Reflecting on the story of his life, he wrote, "I was young then and so much in love with God. I would have done anything for him. That's how I got into preaching in the first place."[19] Suddenly his story took over. His hand flew over the paper, but it could hardly keep up with the story that gushed from his soul and flowed through his ballpoint pen. *Story has its own pace*, he thought. *Story hurries the mind and heart. Stories tell themselves, and all the storyteller can do is try to keep up.* Suddenly Sam could see why storytelling preachers held people's attention. It was because they lost control of themselves and, like the audience before them, were lost in the wonder of the Spirit's great once-upon-a-time.

That Monday night, Sam dreamed a strange dream. He dreamed of Emma Johnson. He often dreamed of Emma Johnson. Sometimes he dreamed the elders had tied her to a

man would take upon himself the task of talking to others in a public place about the most intimate things of the soul.

Perhaps that is why a normal man resents the mention of religion by a stranger and regards as impudent any inquiry on an unexpected occasion concerning his relationship with God. "Who gave you the right," he seems to say, "to put that question to me?"[54]

There is only one answer to any issue of preaching. Our authority to do what we do and say what we say comes from beyond us. It is for precisely that reason that it is to be heeded.

20. Preaching is to change. To give that up is to abandon God's agenda with his world. God wants things changed. Frank Honeycutt writes:

The preacher's role in this labored transformation is not only to speak of his or her own "death" at times (and signs of such should be obvious by the way a preacher now lives), but to be sure the power of God's word to kill and raise people is not softened or diminished. Daniel Berrigan once said, "A Christian should be prepared to look good on wood." The gospel is good news, but depending on your perspective, such news may actually sound pretty bad. So a central role for the preacher is to get a sense for the message, faithfully speak it, and then get out of the way. Death is at work and there may be casualties.[55]

21. All of this imagery about the Second Coming should serve to illustrate to the preacher who wants to be relevant that Second Coming imagery is always interesting but often somewhat remote, and is therefore not always very useful in sermons or, above all, in the lives of parishioners. Keith Nickle says that Jesus' preaching on the end times was intended not so much to give hearers a *Late Great Planet Earth* buzz but to teach them the importance of obedience in seasons of desperation. I have not much use for Second Coming sermons that merely want to explain how—in the preacher's view—the drama of the end is to be celebrated. Give me instead that steadier view of the end times that speaks of God's sovereignty over my life and history as well. Nickle writes:

tree in the forest and then blindfolded her. He thrilled in these lovely dreams to hear her screaming as he preached repentance directly into her ears. He woke up from such dreams smiling into the darkness. He knew they wouldn't change her. He didn't really care so much about preaching for change; that was a seminary idea. Lately he was into preaching for revenge.[20]

His dream was apocalyptic as well. In it, Sister Johnson, with a highly sprayed, Pentecostal beehive hairdo, rode astride a great beast that came up out of the sea. The beast had seven horns, and across its head was written "Trigger!" She was drunk with the blood of cable evangelists, and she was holding up her arms while the seven great bracelets fell toward her shoulder. And an angel sounded his trumpet and cried to the four corners of the sea, "Change not thy sermon style. Beware Emma Johnson, that great harlot of Magog homiletics and the deceiver of the nations." "Fat cow of Bashan," muttered Sam and added, "thou hussie of the apostasy!" Then the beast shot out fire, and hailstones weighing eighty talents fell repeatedly on his overhead projector. And three frogs, like alliterated sermon points, came up out of the Euphrates and croaked in loud godless ribbits, waking Sam up.[21]

Straightening his pajamas and brushing back his unkempt hair, Sam walked briskly to his desk. He loved studying in the early morning hours long before it was time to leave for church. Once more he tried to smooth his unruly hair and

Luke artfully balanced a sense of the immediacy of end-time vividness and drama while at the same time urging his hearers to moderate their frenzied yearning for the climactic culmination of "this age" to approach rapidly. He was not interested in providing a schedule of events to come that would enable his community to chart the progressive approach to the time of the end. He wanted to provoke from within his community confidence and assurance for faithful obedience in the face of the tough demands both of the present and of the future.[56]

22. I wrote in *Spirit, Word, and Story:*

Dabar! How can one word be an event? "Let there be light" is only one word in the original, and yet this verbal economy is precedent to all of Newtonian theory. When God's Holy Spirit moved upon men of old, they did not rattle on with an easy flow of words. They chose, ever so slowly, and etched their vellum scrolls with event. The Ten Commandments are only ten words in the original. Many of the outstanding biblical events come packaged in word thrift.[57]

then picked up his Bible. He reread the Corinthian passages on preaching. He discovered an interesting difference between the first and the ninth chapters of 1 Corinthians. In the first chapter, Paul used the word *kerusso* or "proclaim" in an exhortational sense. But in the ninth chapter, the apostle used the word *euangelizomai*, "to evangelize or preach the good news." It also became clear to him that the Jews found Jesus *skandalon* or "stumbling block," but to the Greeks he was mere *sophia*, "wisdom," which really meant—for most of them—dialectic philosophy. What the Jews tripped over, the Greeks found only a discussion.

Preaching had been hard not only for Sam. It had been the dividing point of the ages. First Corinthians 1:21 talked about the *morias tou kerugmatou*, the "foolishness of preaching." The contrast between *sophia* and *dunamis* in 1 Corinthians 1:24 was a settled matter for Sam. God for him was a verb, the source of *dunamis* and direct action. He had always liked the Hebrew noun for the word, *dabar*.[22] *Dabar* was the "word as event." Whatever God said, happened. *Dunamis* was the changing energy of all that God was in his being. So he preferred *kerussso* above *didache*, for *kerusso*, the "exhortation of energy," was the way God is. *Didache* was teaching; it had to do with the communication of information. It was the learning side of the sermon more than the passion side. It enlightened more than it inquired. Preaching was not so much to enlighten as it was to change. Still, he had to admit that his

23. Both preachers and parishioners too often view inspiration and education as being enemies. On the contrary, they are close friends. It is exciting to learn new things. There is a glorious inspiration in merely learning new facts. These two kinds of truth become indistinguishable in the best of sermons. Says Leanne Payne, "The Incarnation is staggering to the mind. That the creator of all worlds yearns to be our Father."[58]

Is such a fact lesson or jubilation, *didache* or *kerusso*? Of course, it is both!

24. People listen when the force of relational integers come to bear on their need as hearers of the Word. People therefore do not listen to propositions as much as they hear soul experience. The best sermons do not disclose facts; the best sermons lay bare the soul of the preacher. For we who preach disclosing facts can never affect others like we might if we disclosed ourselves. Craig Loscalzo writes:

> Another way to create interesting sermons is to avoid propositional preaching. Such propositions talk about the gospel. . . . There is a difference between preaching about Christ crucified and preaching Christ crucified. The former provides the hearers with more information; the latter transforms the hearers with the power of the gospel.[59]

own affair with the overhead projector was definitely *didache*. In all honesty, he was a good bit more *sophia* than *dabar*. Suddenly he realized he confessed his faith out of the *kerusso* but preached it out of the *didache*.[23]

All of a sudden Sam was ready to make his preaching the demonstration of *dunamis* (1 Cor. 1:18) that Jews enjoyed. He wanted his preaching to be a *semeia* (1 Cor. 1:22), a sign so visible, so demanding, and so life changing that it would challenge Sister Johnson right into the arms of a better attitude.

As he wrote the simple tale of his call to preach, he thought, *Why, there must be at least twenty different words in the New Testament for preaching*. There were the *mattateuo* derivatives that had to do with discipling. The *didache* words that had to do with teaching. The *kerusso* words that had to do with exhorting. There were *katangelo*, *euangelo*, and *laleo*. There were the *katacumen* words that had to do with things like instructing converts. But the word that went best with overhead transparencies would have to be the *didache* words. The word that didn't go as well was *kerusso*, the noun form of which was *kerygma*. Now here was a more Mark Twain kind of a Greek word. It was a word that depended upon good eye contact and congregational oneness to motivate people to listen.[24] It was the work of holding an audience without a rope—or an overhead projector. It was the kind of Greek word not to be found on Microsoft PowerPoint spellchecker.

25. Paul would have been more likely to use PowerPoint than Jesus, since precept-driven preaching would more logically fit the form. If Sam's love for PowerPoint has anything going for it, it must be this: we live in a culture in which the importance of doctrine that might be taught in a sermon is slipping. There can be little question of the value of PowerPoint in those sermons such as might be preached on a Sunday or Wednesday night. These are times when the church would do well to do more logically driven and information-filled sermons. Such sermons would teach people to think in more structured and theological ways. Doctrine is important, and PowerPoint sermons have a definite *didache* possibility for this mode of preaching. James Thompson writes:

> William Hendricks, after interviewing people to find out why they left churches, encourages pastors to teach people to think theologically, so they can resist what is essentially "Mc-doctrine"—spiritual fast food of proof-texts and clichés that are filling and fattening but not particularly nourishing.[60]

Then a chilling thought came to Sam. It should have come to him earlier, but it never had. Which of those Greek words would best describe the teachings of Jesus? Would it be *didache* or *kerygma?* Sam felt bad that it would probably be *kerygma.* Jesus seemed to him a little more Garrison Keillor than the ponderous, point-making precept prophet. But where did all this alliterative outlining come from? He had to admit it seemed to be missing from the Sermon on the Mount as well as Paul's sermon on Mars Hill. It seems to have been rooted in popular evangelical styles and no older than the nineteenth century at most. In fact, what really troubled Sam was that the church had lived apparently for nineteen centuries without it.

Then came the most chilling question of his entire homiletics career: would Jesus have used an overhead projector and PowerPoint?[25] A good question! It was also a moot question—moot since he would have had no place to plug it in. Oh, of course, Jesus would surely have used one for the praise choruses, else how would all those new disciples who couldn't read hymnbooks ever join in? But what about his sermons?

Sam looked over at his watch. Whoa! It was time he got dressed and headed for the church. He jumped up, threw off his pajamas, and got dressed. Still the question of whether Jesus would have used PowerPoint troubled Sam for the rest of the day. He just kept thinking of his Lord in his Sunday

26. Sam, obviously, is writing a confessional sermon—a testimonial homily—which is the most interesting of all sermon forms. The power of self-disclosure makes such preaching riveting. For a while, advocates of the New Homiletic were encouraging preachers not to use themselves as illustrations in their preaching. Nothing, of course, could be more wrong. "I" is a powerful pronoun. It can be abused, but when the preacher uses the term with discretion and forethought, it is not only legitimate; it is preferred. The opening lines of Barbara Brown Taylor's *The Luminous Web* read:

> I am not a scientist. It is true that I received a small microscope for my ninth birthday and gave myself headaches by looking into it for hours at a time. The first thing I saw was a hair plucked from my own head, as fat and shiny as a tarred telephone pole. After that, I tried everything that would fit below the eyepiece: flower petals, dirt, a page torn from the telephone book. I spent the better part of an afternoon with a dropper full of pond water, and—once I had worked up my nerve—with a smear of my own blood that was as beautiful to me as a red stained glass window.[61]

Reading such a passage, I realize that it pulls me in because it is good description, but I think mostly it ties me up in interest because I am a fan of Dr. Brown Taylor and I now know more about her than I did before she included a bit of herself in her presentation. Naturally, people feel the same way about their pastor. They genuinely want to know him or her. The use of the self in an illustration is not generally abusive but the furthering of a relationship.

27. By this time, Sam has realized that ordination symbolizes the empowering of the Spirit. That empowering stands first at our ordination, but it must attend every sermon ever to be preached after that. Why? Because as Donald Coggan reminds us:

> When true preaching takes place, the main actor is not the preacher, nor the congregation but the Holy Spirit. . . . Without him and creative and recreative activity, there can be words, there can be essays, there can be the reading of a paper, but there can be no preaching.[62]

toga trying to get his sermon disk in the A-floppy drive. When he was finally settled in his study at church, Sam went back to writing the story of his call to preach.

Sam worked throughout the following week on his sermon. He felt a new kind of nonalliterative thrill as he worked up a brand-new kind of sermon. He wrote the story of his call to preach and how he had felt the thrill of knowing that God wanted him to do this.[26] It was a riveting story that began with the death of a high school chum that forever marked his life with this question: what should life be used for? The story then passed through a knee injury he had suffered in college while on the football team that shut him out of the conference championship. He then talked about the most grueling challenge of all: his self-doubts about his ability to communicate and that awful neurosis surrounding his first sermon.

When all of these crises were passed, his story wound down to the cliff-hanging conclusion of how he met God in the gravity of his ordination and how, when the elders laid their hands on him, he felt the incarnation power of the Savior.[27]

He had no more dreams that week, but on Wednesday night, he did have to lead the Brigadeers, a boys' camping group. He hated having to do it, because he just didn't relate to kids. Even when he tried to get things down to their simplest level, that smart alec Tommy Jenkins would always disturb his talk by asking what supralapsarian meant.

28. Preaching done well lures those weary with a meaningless vocation to wish they might actually be what they behold. The children who are moved by Sam's sermon see in the words the answer to the greatest question the sermon can answer: Is God among us or not? William Willimon says:

> Whenever we gather on Sunday, that is still our question. Is the Lord among us or not (Ex. 17:7)? We thought that our problem was our need for freedom, for liberation. No. Our problem is thirst. Our controversy is over appropriate ways to quench thirst. And every Sunday the preacher strikes the rock and there is water, things are brought to speech, and silence is broken. The Lord is with us.[63]

It is a most attractive calling when the keepers of the water tell a thirsty world where to get a drink. No wonder preaching well done is God's recruiting office.

As he walked into the group, one of the children asked him how he had come to be a preacher, and Sam started to tell him. He hadn't gotten very far into the story when his sermon preparation began to take over. He told the tale of his call to preach, and the children moved in and were utterly fascinated. When he got all through, Tommy Jenkins, who always asked Sam a lot of questions, had only one for him. "Wow! Pastor Sam, do you think I could ever become a preacher like you?"

Sam smiled. "Maybe you could be a preacher," he said. But in his heart, he wouldn't wish that upon anybody, ever, and particularly upon little children.[28]

"Not me," said Billy Simmons. "I don't want to be a preacher. Preachers are always fat and bald, and they talk too long."

Sam smiled again, then ground his teeth. "Let me tell you another story about Elisha and what happened to some children who called him a fat baldie!" He didn't tell that story, but he really wanted to. It sure must have been more fun preaching in the old Bible days when those who mocked preachers could be attacked by she-bears. Now, when she-bears attacked preachers, they got a lot of support from personnel committees.

Thursday morning, he continued refining his new narrative sermon.

Of course, he knew that many would scoff at it. There would be all kinds of recipients of the gospel. To the Jews, there would be the necessity of power, then preaching would

Notations

29. No wonder the New Homiletic turns somewhat on Craddock's title *Overhearing the Gospel*. David Buttrick provides a sidewise glance at the power of all story when he evaluates the stories of Jesus:

> They may be designed for a kind of group conversion. Parables usually begin rather tritely, depicting our everyday world in an everyday way, but then in most cases there is something surreal that disrupts our world, and hints at a wider more mysterious world—as well as a more astonishing God. . . . If I am correct, then speaking in parables is a tricky, exciting craft.[64]

30. Calvin Miller, *Spirit, Word, and Story*.[65]

31. Miller, *Spirit, Word, and Story*.[66]

32. Miller, *Spirit, Word, and Story*.[67]

33. Calvin Miller, *The Empowered Communicator*.[68]

be a window full of light. To the Greeks, there would be the
necessity of content and much relevant, practical wisdom. The
Jews demanded that the sermon interest and inspire, and the
Greeks that it inform and educate. But this was the best part
of the *narratio;* it would do both. *Narratio* was indirect.[29]

Søren Kierkegaard long ago said, "It also became clear to
me that if I desired to communicate anything ... it would first
of all be necessary to give my exposition an indirect form."
Bruno Bettelheim wrote, "Fairie stories are 'spiritual explo-
rations' and hence 'the most life-like' since they reveal 'human
life as seen, or felt, or divined from the inside.'"[30] F. Dean
Lueking wrote, "Preaching the biblical word today cannot
take on a peopleless monotone when such a story of people's
stories is its authority."[31] And Allan Bloom wrote, "Without
literature ... the fine art of comparison is lost."[32] Sam was
beginning to realize that a sermonic story could do some wonderful things for preaching that his alliterative slides could not
do. He remembered an old English teacher quoting the novel-
ist F. Scott Fitzgerald: "Draw your chair up close to the edge
of the precipice and I'll tell you a story."[33] He thought of how
thrilling it would be to have Mrs. Johnson on the edge of a
precipice.

Under the spell of this new truth, the rest of the week
flew by and suddenly it was Sunday morning. It was then,
quite early, that Sam got cold feet. He suddenly felt that his
people would not understand him if he pulled such a radically

34. Trying new sermon styles and approaches is the scariest of all ventures. Yet Richard F. Ward tells us why this is a great idea for all of us who must speak in the midst of an entertainment culture, a culture which Neil Postman characterized as amusing itself to death. Ward says:

> Not only does the sermon in performance make a "self" and a "world," it also unmakes them. The sermon is a site for performance where the preacher may enter a free space created for serious play and unmask established orders and structures.[69]

No wonder Sam prefers the safety of older forms; the stakes are far less high than the high tension and gasping ecstasy of new forms.

different pulpit style on them. He was afraid to try the narrative approach. He suddenly felt that while it worked for some, it would never work for him. He thought he would appear inept and foolish, that he would embarrass himself in some unnatural form that he should never have tried in the first place. His resolve dissolved in nonresolve. He doubted the dangerous just before he regressed once more into the comfortable.[34]

He flew early to his study and quickly outlined his twenty-sixth sermon on Romans. Romans 14. "Oh yes, thank you, God! Give me back my PowerPoint and my old way of doing things. Help me to continue my strong teaching and stem the tide of human apostasy. Even so, come quickly, Lord Jesus," Sam breathed as his fingers flew at the keys of his computer. In but minutes, the beast retreated. The great harlot of narrative preaching, that Jezebel of Omri, retreated into her dark corner and was chained for a thousand years. "Out of my life, you narrative Gog from the abyss of Magog." Sam selected "print" and pushed the key. "Mother of harlots, be chained!" Sam screamed. His fingers urged his computer mouse to "select." "Now Narratio is damned and the apostasy is stanched! Now comes the White Rider armed with PowerPoint transparencies. Back to the river, ye vile frogs of the Euphrates!" Sam pushed "enter." The computer whirred and the whirlwind spit out a lovely four-inch floppy full of Sam's customary fiery font. Armed with his Bible in

35. So far I have never met a soul who will call herself a liberal. It is a word that no preacher will own up to. But theology has been seriously weakened by those who somehow have forgotten to teach it in ways that apply the strength of Scripture to the needs of the hearer. Postmodern preaching has accommodated the virile definitions of the Bible to what people think they want in a sermon. At least Sam is not guilty of that. Buttrick writes:

> In a recent Doonesbury cartoon panel, a church-shopping young couple is appalled to hear a preacher use the word "sinner." "We're looking for a church that's supportive, a place where we can feel good about ourselves," the young wife explains.[70]

Whether or not Pastor Sam is overreacting, he is at least concerned that the Scripture does exist to shape the church rather than the other way around.

one hand, Sam grabbed the disk in the other and started off toward the sanctuary. The Quixote of Exegesis with the software of salvation, the disk of deliverance, the Pentium of leviathan. He would storm the plains of Megiddo and drive the dragon back into the fire pit.

"Narratio be cast into Gehenna, along with the thousand liberal preachers who told little stories in the great falling away of the church!"[35]

And thus it came to pass that Sam Quixote de la Mancha set off to tilt at the mills of modernism, to preach the true Word as God intended it to be preached.

Sam happened to be passing the vestibule just as Mrs. Johnson came in.

"Good morning, pastor!" She snipped her words. "Are our little slides on Romans 14 lying eagerly on the overhead? I believe this is sermon twenty-six. You know what that means . . . in only four more sermons, you'll have to ruin the pleasure we are currently finding in some other book of the Bible you haven't yet overexplained."

"Good morning, Mrs. Johnson," Sam greeted her without answering the issue.

The organist began to play and the thin choir consisting of a Clairol soprano, two nasal altos, and three Geritol bassos filed in and took six chairs in an Amish gender arrangement. The service went on in its customary fashion until it was time for the sermon. Just as Sam was standing up to preach, a tall

man in sunglasses and a trench coat entered and hurriedly sat down by Mrs. Johnson in the fourth row. Although Sam had not seen him since Monday, it was clearly Sermoniel. Sam couldn't believe it! Sunglasses! Why was he being so obvious in his attempt to be incognito? His presence at first made Sam feel as though the archangel was just showing up to grade his papers for the day.

Sam watched as Emma Johnson leaned toward Sermoniel. He had no idea what she was saying to him, but it seemed pleasant enough.

What Emma said was simply, "Good morning! It's nice to have you in church. Are you from around here?"

"Not right around here. I just flew in for the service."

"Oh, are you a frequent flier?"

"Well . . . you might say that!"

"I'm Emma Johnson. I come here because I'm just nuts about overhead projectors. How about you?"

"Well, I'm into more homiletic movement and story-oriented sermons."

"This could be a long service for you. We all love projector sermons around here."

Sam read a few verses from Romans 14 and then said, "Today, my sermon is titled 'Deliverance: The Desperate Doctrine of Delight.'"

"Our pastor has the gift of alliteration." Emma smiled.

36. Why are some sermons considered to be powerful and some not? I suspect it all has to do with a hearing factor. If the congregation believes that the sermon cares about their needs, they will listen. If they believe that the sermon has met their needs, they will judge it to be powerful. J. Philip Wogaman writes: "It is easy to forget that the sermon that counts is not the one that is written but the one that is heard."[71]

"Maybe not," said Sermoniel. Sam walked over to the projector. He put his slides down on the little shelf and reached for the switch and flipped it on.

But the projector bulb that was to stem the armies of the east, and then the apostasy, didn't come on. Sam checked the wall plug to be sure that it was plugged in. It was. "Would one of you men go and check the breaker panel? We're not getting any power here," said Sam.

"Believe me," Emma whispered to Sermoniel, "it's been quite a spell since we've had any power here."[36]

After a moment, there was a fluttering of the sanctuary lights and the stopping and starting of the air conditioner, indicating that someone somewhere was running through the breakers. But no solution could be found. In this moment of debilitation and utter terror, Sam suddenly smiled and then turned his eyes toward the ceiling and prayed the kind of prayer small gladiators once prayed in the arena.

"My dearly beloved. Technology being what it is, I have decided to preach in a different manner." Sam read his two passages from 1 Corinthians, prayed his pastoral prayer, and launched out boldly into his sermon.

"Today I want to tell you a story. It is the story of one of the electric moments of my adolescence. I cannot tell you this tale without starting at the point of one of the most difficult moments of my life ... the death of a very close friend."

37. In the last analysis, when people really listen to a sermon, it probably has very little to do with forms and techniques formally learned. David P. Mulder suggests:

> I have a high respect for seminary education. Pastors need the preparatory work it provides. Far too often, however, in the academic atmosphere the student writes sermons to please the professor, who is usually a scholar. Many seminary students also personally identify with their professors. They hear the professor lecture day after day. It should come as no surprise when a new preacher sounds much like a professor during the first years of ministry.[72]

When a pastor learns to grip the audience's mind, he is generally playing by a more personal, relational, and mystical set of rules than the seminary was able to teach.

Sam then preached his first narrative sermon. The Corinthian text wound its way through the various episodes of his affair with preaching. But the further the tale went, the more Sam was aware that the people were on the edge of their seats with a rapport he had never before experienced. The narrative was so emotional that some were nearly in tears as the sermon reached its conclusion. Something new was born between the preacher and his people. Something very powerful was standing at the center of their community that welded them in a special oneness they had never felt before.[37]

But best of all, Sam, who had reformed the heart of his sermon in his first encounter with God, had in this last encounter found its heart. God was the author of a great story, and the story was to be doled out chapter by chapter in the weekly sermon. Stories flew on spirit wings—God's story, Sam's story, the hearers' stories—all seemed to gather beneath the Spirit's keeping as the soaring stories created God's kingdom right before Sam's eyes and in the very presence of the *narratio*.

After the benediction, Sam went to the back door of the church. Some were still so moved at the power of his narrative exposition that they spoke only brief, quiet courtesies as they left the building. But Emma Johnson was rarely moved to an extent that left her without words. "Well, Sam, that was quite a sermon."

"Why thank you, my dear," said Sam.

"I suppose next week we'll be back on sermon twenty-six on Romans 14."

After a long silence, Sam said, "Can I tell you that not until this past hour have I known the sheer grip of terror and the ecstasy of preaching? It isn't in the customary that the terror is born, nor perhaps the potential. Somehow, I fear the next intermingling of such a time, but I'm not sure I ever want to live without this psychotic ecstasy ever again."

"Oh, pastor," Emma cooed, "I wonder if in your fear and trembling there isn't some kind of possibility for both yourself and this congregation."

They shook hands, and Sam watched Emma and Sermoniel walk out into the sunlight.

Once Sam could hear them no longer, Emma turned toward Sermoniel. "You know, the Lord does work in strange ways, don't you think?"

"He sure does." Sermoniel pulled his hand out of his trench-coat pocket and opened his hand. There in the middle of it lay a small glass object.

"Is that what I think it is?" Emma asked. "Is it a projector bulb?"

Sermoniel winked. Emma Johnson laughed.

"In such a little thing is a whole world of God's glory," said Emma. "Coming back to church next week?"

She turned to wait for Sermoniel's reply, but he was gone.

"You *are* a frequent flier" was all she said.

She noticed that on the sidewalk lay the projector bulb. "I guess they don't need that in heaven," she mused as she bent over and picked it up. "Shall I take it back to the church and put it in the projector?" she asked herself. She shook her head and smiled and let the bulb fall to the sidewalk. Then she placed her Cuban heel on the bulb and crushed it into a thousand glittering shards of sunlight.

"Here's to next Sunday!" she laughed and added looking up into the sky, "God bless Sam in the lonely journey he has begun."

It was a beautiful afternoon and too lovely to admit that if the great apostasy of the last days really had begun, it could never be Sam's fault.

1. The symbol at the heart of this story is every visitor's protective privacy. People come to church seeking and yet fearing relationships. They want anonymity, and yet they don't. Bill Hybels calls his "seekers" "anonymous Harry and Mary." But in merely visiting a church for the first time, people have some desire to end their anonymity in friendship. Still, they want to be invited rather than forced into the fellowship. Sermoniel's aloofness sets him off as a visitor who wants to remain apart. Yet here is the glory of preaching, particularly narrative preaching. It breaks down our separateness as the attention we give the sermon makes us one. But sermons are bonding servants. Open sermons create rapt attention and dissolve audience separation in intense rapport. When the Spirit fully occupies the sermon, audience unity is mandatory. Donald Coggan was an advocate of such sermons:

> *Grant, O God,*
> *That I may speak so boldly*
> *And so lovingly*
> *That the greatness of Christ*
> *May shine out clearly in my person,*
> *Through the indwelling of your Holy Spirit.*[73]

THREE

GATHERING THE SERMON FROM THE ARENA OF LIFE

In the spinning of the days, Sam's church began to grow. He had managed to couple his need for God with an exciting form of narrative exposition. Fire and interest had met in a new atmosphere of joy. Sam was preaching. The congregation was listening. It was the way things should be in church. They were doing blended worship—a little Beethoven, a little bongo; a little hype, a little Haydn; and a lot of 2x, 3x choruses before a seventeenth-century anthem. Some of the music was ethereal, some athletic. But overall it seemed inspirational, except when it didn't.

Emma found herself seated once again by Sermoniel, the Angel of Homiletics, although she still had no idea who he was. But she had wondered about his odd demeanor, for every time she saw him at church, he was dressed in a trench coat and wore sunglasses.[1] She

2. Vitality and interest should be the best of friends. Neither of them go anyplace without the other. Further, only as sermons become relevant with information that is highly useful to the majority of the congregation will the sermon inspire them to listen at all. Rick Ezell writes:

> When the Barna Research group asked unchurched people what might bring them into a church, the number one response (given by nearly one out of five) was better messages. I suspect that what they meant by better messages was sermons that spoke to them where they lived and that addressed their pressing needs. People want Christian public speakers to know them personally, to empathize with their hurts, and to revel in their joys. Such messages are practical, for they teach people their similarity each to the other.[74]

3. All audiences are hungry for important truths, and in their minds, all important truths have to do with meaning. Every preacher should ask himself, "Am I telling important truths? Are my words full of significance for each of my hearers? If not, why am I preaching this?" It would be better not to preach at all than to preach merely because it is time for the sermon. Every great sermon must grapple with meaning. David Buttrick writes:

> I view ministry as a vocation of meaning. Ministers are meaning-givers not merely for a parish, but in everything ministers do everywhere. All of which means that ministers must study every day of their lives. They can. They can because lay people can manage churches very well, design programs, write church newspapers, and all the rest. Lay people are also excellent at giving comfort, visiting the sick and helping in other wonderful ways. Ministers can assist in giving meaning to programs, and deep meaning to desperate people in crisis moments. These days ministers are beset; too many demands assail them. But they may be dodging their primary concern—meaning![75]

still marveled over his instantaneous coming and going, but his angelic status had never occurred to her. But he grinned too much to her way of thinking. She found it desperately hard to feel spiritual in church seated by a grinning man in a trench coat.

He turned her way and kept the grin going.

"Stop doing that!" she said, half aloud. But he kept right on.

Then Emma gave a little startled cough as he spoke to her. "Do you think Sam means all that stuff he's saying or is he just preaching?"

Emma smiled and then whispered, "Well, at least he's no longer boring."

"No, but he's not very vital either. He isn't convincing me that he really means what he is saying."[2]

Emma turned the idea over in her mind.

Sam went right on preaching.

Sermoniel went right on talking. "His arrival at story-telling has made him more interesting, but it can't supply him with fire. The man needs more passion about what he's talking about if he's going to convince me he believes what he's talking about. He's cute! He's clever! He's just not inflamed with any important truth."[3]

Sermoniel stopped and grinned even broader. Then he turned more fully toward Emma—as fully as the pew

4. Some years ago, I wrote an article titled "Neural Linguistics Make Lingual Neurotics." The import of the article was to remind preachers that certain words are trigger words to specific individuals within an audience. The word *father* is a great word for most, but not for those who have been raised by abusive parents. The entire politically correct movement is about the issue of neural linguistics. How do we speak so that we keep everyone listening? We must be careful to avoid using these trigger words or phrases. Emma Johnson's objection to Sam's use of a synonym for donkey is more common in conservative churches than might at first seem reasonable. I remember in a sermon on guilt quoting some words from Lady Macbeth's famous soliloquy "Out, damned spot!" One dear sister stopped me after church to tell me that quoting Shakespeare's famed femme fatale was all right but that whatever Shakespeare had her say, I should have had her say something more appropriate, like "Oh fiddlesticks!" I burst out laughing at her suggestion, but her offense at my laughter was only second to her offense at my use of the Shakespearean quote. What I learned was that nearly everybody has some neural linguistic trigger that is easy to trip. It does not mean that we should change every word which might offend, but it does mean that we need a growing conscience about what should be stricken from our sermons because of impropriety or political incorrectness.

would permit—and really grinned as he began to fade out of sight.

"Stop doing that!" Emma insisted, but far too loudly. Several around her in the pews looked in her direction. He had almost completely faded away, except for his impish grin, which widened in spite of her rebuke. Then it faded and was gone.

As he finished the sermon, Sam tried to think of another way to leave the church building, one that would avoid his having to pass Mrs. Johnson. But Emma had already caught his eye, and having been seen, he knew there was no way to avoid passing her. She was leaning against the white jamb of the vestry doors as Sam approached.

"Sam," she said, "could we talk about your preaching?"

"Emma. Hello! Yes, of course! I was just saying to myself, 'I hope Emma wants to talk about my preaching. Her spiritual gift is sermon evaluation.'"

"Well, Sam," said Emma, "I like your new narrative style of preaching. It's so much more interesting. But your sermon on Balaam's ... well ... the word *donkey* would have been more appropriate. And when you were reading from the Epistles, you used the word *dung*. Isn't there another word for that?"[4]

"Yes, there is, but you wouldn't like that one either."

5. Perhaps what Emma is really trying to say is that every sermon needs to have that feeling that it has not come from the preacher's creativity or the lexicon or even the Bible per se. It needs to feel as though it has come from God. The motive for every sermon should be the same: Does God want this said? Loving Jesus is the motive for obedience in all things—certainly in sermon writing. The sermon has a better chance of finding its source and being in God if the preacher also feels this is her source as well. Donald Coggan puts it this way:

> When true preaching takes place, the main actor is not the preacher, nor the congregation but the Holy Spirit. That he uses men and women as his agents and fellow workers is true, and we shall have more to say about this shortly. But it is essential that we grasp the fact that, when an act of real preaching takes place, the most active part, the most vital part of the enterprise is taken by the third person of the Trinity. Without him and his creative and recreative activity, there can be words, there can be essays, there can be the "reading of a paper," but there can be no preaching.[76]

6. One of the difficulties that every person of God faces in our day of Second Coming novels is how to keep a proper perspective. These simply written novels have furnished the West—both the religious and the secular West—with a dramatic worldview and a popularized eschatology. So many people cherish their novelized worldview to the point that they feel they are quasi scholars on the subject. They have not enough study of the Second Coming to know much about it; they only feel that their view—the popular, premillennial view—is the right one. So they often put their pastor's view on trial, checking his orthodoxy against their own. It is important for the pastor to temper this new bourgeois theology with his better studies and less glitzy views of the end of time. Keith Nickle reminds us:

> Luke emphasizes keeping vigil for Jesus's return by sustaining the quality of one's discipleship rather than seeking to calculate the most likely moment for his appearance and then waiting till then to prepare. Energies expended over computations about the calendar and sequences of end-of-time events are futile and counterproductive. They divert attention from faithful witness through ministry and self-spending service to the

"Well, Sam, your new narrative style of exposition is sometimes riveting ..."

"But?"

"But, it is ... well ..." Emma paused as though she was fishing for some tactful way to go on, and then she just blurted out, "Sam ... do you love Jesus or not?"[5]

The statement was abrupt! Emma was always abrupt. In fact, Sam believed that the word *Emma* came from an old Germanic word that meant "abrupt." But he went into a temporary state of shock because Emma had been so up-front with him. It took him a moment to cope.

"Well, yes, of course, Emma, I love Jesus; oh, I'm sure I don't love him like you do—I could never aspire to such spiritual excellence—but I do love him."

Emma smiled. "Well, I don't know if I would use the term 'spiritual excellence'; I only know my friends tell me I am certainly deep in my devotion. You know, Sam, I believe in going all the way with my faith. I'm an all-or-nothing sort of girl. I'm big on commitment, but modesty is by far my strongest asset. I know that you can tell how much I detest spiritual shallowness. I don't know if you're aware of this, pastor, but most of your members have never read a single Second Coming novel. It's the kind of spiritual darkness that will characterize the end times. Have you, Sam? Have you read a Second Coming novel?"[6]

believer's devoted anticipation to the certain completion of God's plan.[77]

Every preacher and every sermon must be aware of theological fads and do all they can to minimize their hold on the congregation. The preacher must ever seek to help a congregation grow into an honest and more studied biblical worldview.

7. Warren Wiersbe has suggested that preachers would be better off to approach the writing of a sermon as a poet approaches the writing of a poem than as a lawyer approaches the writing of a brief. If this is true (and it must be), then the preacher would see homiletics more as an art than a science. Christopher Marlowe's Dr. Faustus admits, "When I behold the heavens I repent" (scene vi, line 2). The arts and the Bible are about the same thing: life. I wonder that they do not more often join forces in a sermon both to fascinate and instruct.

Anna Akhmatova in her marvelous poem "Obverse" writes:

> *I dreamt that I was held to*
> *Creating a libretto for music that flowed evermore,*
> *And a dream is something substantial,*
> *The bluebird the soft embalmer,*
> *The ramparts of Elsinore.*[78]

If art were not necessary in heralding the Word of God, would God have written much of the Bible in poetry? Perhaps he felt the world was too prosaic and gave preachers the responsibility of washing its drab prose with the brush of homiletics dipped in the pigment of all things beautiful—the arts.

8. Passion is born when the heaviness of what the preacher has to say gets married to his or her need to get it said. "Becoming an effective teacher is simple," said Marlene LeFever. "You just prepare and prepare until little drops of blood appear on your forehead."[79]

Passion therefore is born when the preacher has something to say and has to say something. Passion is that definite feeling that if I don't get this message out, God will think less of me, my audience will be unfurnished, and I will not be able to live with the notion that the words of my sermon were not significant.

Sam ducked his head and blushed. It was clear to Emma that Sam was also not into the deeper life movement.

"Sam, you know what Dr. LeStraw says? He says that those who will not stand in front could be left behind. But then maybe your reluctance to study these deeper things is your answer to my original question."

"You mean the question of whether I love Jesus?"

"Exactly. You see, your new story-oriented style has given you a new power in the pulpit. I'm sure you've noticed that the eleven o'clock service is SRO."

"SRO?"

"It's a term from the arts—from Broadway; it means 'standing room only.' There's no way I could expect you to be familiar with the arts, having spent most of your life in a seminary.[7] But Sam, while the art of preaching is enhanced by good narrative style, it still comes second to the preacher's passion. Storytelling may hold our attention, but it can never really change us. No, Sam, the force that a sermon needs to change a congregation has to come from the preacher's passion."[8]

Emma had a way of sounding like his old homiletics professor. She was making some sense, but Sam knew he mustn't let on. He must not ever let her think she was right. She would be merciless if he showed any weakness. So he pretended to be her preaching pupil for a moment.

9. How do we quicken our homiletic nervous system? By working at being human. Humans feel and touch life as they move through it. Sermons become human as sermonizers drop their fear of the world and embrace it for its warm lessons. When Barbara Brown Taylor was asked what advice she would give to a preacher, she said:

> That's easy. Increase your life. Live your life more fully. And pay attention to it. . . . Stay as alive as you dare, and trust that your life with all its unorthodox twists and turns is still God's territory. Dare to tell some stories that don't sound like religious stories. Use some language that doesn't sound like it belongs in church. Read fiction. Take clogging lessons. Go be alive, so that you yourself are a living sermon about abundant life. Then whatever you say will be worth listening to.[80]

Everything I read by this remarkable woman of God convinces me that she serves up her sermons never forgetting that preaching has a nervous system.

10. Emma Johnson is right about this. Preaching that exists only to fascinate usually ends up being only cute or boring. Preaching exists to call the world Godward, and if a sermon does not do that, it ceases to be a sermon in the strictest sense of the word. James Thompson reminds us that preaching has a multifold task in the life of the church:

> Christian preaching involves an authoritative word from God that is mediated by the preacher. It shapes the consciousness of the listeners and leads them in a doxology of prayer and praise. Preaching initiates the listeners in a new grammar of faith in which the congregation learns the words of prayer, praise and doxology. Preaching also creates and sustains a community consciousness in which individuals come to recognize that their identity cannot be separated from the corporate identity of the church.[81]

Preaching has much to do. We dare not reduce it to entertainment.

"And just how do I get this passion?"

"Well, you'll have to figure that out, but it seems to me that the location of passion is to be found in the same place as the answer to the original question."

"The question of whether I love Jesus."

"Sam, story exposition can move the congregation closer to the pulpit, but the object of great preaching is to move the congregation closer to God. Great preaching doesn't just orate. Great preaching feels! Homiletics has a nervous system.[9] It thrills the listener as it approaches God; it weeps when it sees others hurting. It's like Jesus. Jesus didn't prove himself the Son of God by drawing big crowds. Pink Floyd did that last week in Cincinnati. Jesus proved himself the Son of God by loving God and weeping over the masses. Sam, when is the last time you've seen anybody weeping in church?"

"Counting the time when Thomas Crunchlaw forgot his glasses and put a hundred-dollar bill in the plate when he thought he was putting in a ten?"

"Well, I'll tell you this, Sam, you need to stop trying to please us by merely interesting us. It is not enough to fascinate us with your sermons. Your sermons need to change us.[10]

"Well, Sam, I'm off to Luella Parsons' Bible study. Now there's a woman who loves Jesus. She's also good at blueberry strudel."

11. Our knowledge and friendship with Christ will prevent us from taking the sermon more seriously than we take our God-affair. For in truth our affair with Christ will determine the validity of our affair with our audience. Further, the sermon just works better when we see it as belonging to God even as we preach it. If we saw the sermon as God's, we would have fewer feelings of failure in the pulpit. We would see ourselves more as stewards of our preachment than as its sole creator and owner. Coggan makes this very point when he says:

> We have all known those dreadful occasions when we have had no comeback from the congregation—the electric stream goes out but does not come back, and there is no enhancement of what the preacher does! The reasons for this deadness may be many. We ourselves may not have been in touch with the Master; or our preparation may have been deficient; or our relationship with others may have been all wrong; all these things block the flow of the current and must be taken into consideration. But sometimes—I believe often—the reason for the deadness is that our people have never been taught that preaching is a function of the church and not simply the "man up there."[82]

"Well, that's pretty much the whole list of Christian virtues."

Emma ignored him.

Then she left. Her absence always came like a breath of fresh air.

Sam was glad to see her go. *What impertinence*, he thought. *How dare she ask if I love Jesus?*

Sam was still thinking about her question that afternoon when he was in his study at home working on his next sermon. Suddenly he heard someone clear his throat behind him in the darkness. At one time, the sinister gurgling would have terrified him, but no longer.

"Hark! Hark, I say! Be not afraid. For it is I—"

"Yeah, I know who it is, and I'm harking. And as for being afraid, you need to know you don't scare me anymore. Okay, Sermoniel. Come on out and show yourself."

Sermoniel, the Angel of Homiletics, emerged from the darkness. "She's right, you know."

"Who's right?"

"Emma Johnson."

"Why do you always take her side in every quarrel?"

"Well, she's right about this. Just writing creative sermons isn't enough. Your flock needs to know and love God. They will neither love him nor get to know him until you show them the way.[11] You're not the big deal, Sam! Jesus Christ is

12. Those preachers who hunger to get their people attached to God are preachers who are at peace with the purpose of preaching. Samuel Proctor wrote:

> The sermon is different from other staged events because it seeks to tilt life Godward, to encourage us to answer as we are addressed by God.[83]

13. What is it that we are to do in the prayer closet that will effect the power and influence of the sermon? William Bouknight says that we might use twenty minutes of our time in that closet to achieve what he calls a four-step recovery of the power of Holy Scripture. Here are Bouknight's suggestions:

> First, as you prepare to open the Bible, pray a few moments for God's inspiration and for understanding.
> Second, read at least five verses. Start with the New Testament and use a modern translation, like the New International Version.
> Three, after you read, ask yourself if there is a truth in what you have read that God wants you to receive and live by.
> Four, thank God for that truth and proceed into a time of prayer.
> These twenty minutes a day can revolutionize your life.[84]

This explains why the closet is relevant in giving power to the sermon, but what of our affair with the people? How is this to be useful? We must live among them. Our Sunday sermon dialogue should be just as people-centered as our lives among our people have been the previous week. It must also be true that we recognize that the people of God have a contribution to make to both our lives and our sermons. Coggan said years ago:

> The people of God, the laity, have much to give. Each member of the body of Christ has a contribution to make. Each has some experience of God's grace coming to them in Christ, the gifts of the Spirit differing from each other in a wide variety. The laity have a knowledge of the world, of men and affairs that the clergy sometimes lack. They know the questions which their friends in business or in the professions or in the shops are actually asking.[85]

the true shepherd of the sheep. Every great sermon is a gallery in which there hangs a single portrait—the portrait of Christ. You're just the undershepherd who brings the sheep to the Master Shepherd. Only that's hard for you to do, and do you know why?"

"Huh uh," muttered Sam.

"Because you haven't been hanging around the Master Shepherd yourself very much. A good preacher brings to the pulpit good sermons from his private devotion. A great preacher brings to the pulpit great sermons from the presence of God. A story-intense sermon makes a really interesting homily. And intense listening addicts listeners to Christ. In fact, it may only addict them to the preacher's creativity. And what preacher was ever that creative? More than that, it can sponsor a kind of psychological weakness in some preachers that keeps them trying to attach people to themselves rather than to God.[12] Preachers were called to preach in such a way as to bring God's presence to the people."

"Well, where is the presence of God; how can I get into it?" Sam felt these questions had such obvious answers that he wished he hadn't asked them.

"Sam, the presence of God has two very different locations. One is in your private adoration of Christ, where you get to know God one on one. The other is in the midst of the people, where he lives.[13]

14. Bouknight reminds us that to seek to build the church just to help pay off the mortgage is the most godless of all reasons to set evangelism into our preaching:

> Today many mainline churches are not calling sinners to be redeemed; they are just rounding up respectable folks to help pay off the mortgage.[86]

Vance Havner has been widely quoted in any number of sermons as saying, "We're building million-dollar launching pads to send up firecrackers."

The great churches usually became great because they could legitimately be accused of saying urgent and important things. Thompson writes:

> Throughout the history of the church, one of the major functions of the sermon has been to provide instruction for the congregation to live the Christian life. Preaching has provided direction for the community, guiding both individuals and the corporate community toward faithful living.[87]

In spite of this important heritage, churches sometimes mumble only an odd sociology driven by casserole affairs and softball leagues.

"Passion feels; it hurts; it bleeds. Without passion, sermons degenerate into pointless points and commentary notes. They are mere gigabytes of information about God without a drop of red blood in them. Sermons should be dangerous, inflamed with hope and terror."

"Whoa there! I don't know if I want to be that. I want to just be a normal guy and get paid to preach and play a little golf on Mondays."

"You're playing it safe, Sam! Too safe! Preachers are not supposed to live safely. Put some orange construction cones and caution signs around your pulpit. Post a sign that says, 'Danger—obedience can be hazardous to your health. Listen to this sermon at your own risk.' Become what you're supposed to be—a messenger of life and death, of salvation and damnation. Too many preachers are bought off with country club memberships and stock options. Then they become what Harriet Beecher Stowe called 'fox-hunting parsons.'[14]

"Great preaching springs from two wells—life among the people and time alone with God. If you would know this great passion, spend time alone with God and spend time in the company of people, where he is ever to be found in abundance.

"Sam, do you know what God's favorite magazine is?"

"*Christianity Today*?"

"Gong! Sorry, Sam, it's *People* magazine. God loves people. He inhabits their pain and laughter. He lives with

15. J. Philip Wogaman has this to say about letting the sermon rise from its natural source among the laity:

> If caring for the congregation is a good principle for effective prophetic preaching, I am not sure it is one that can be followed for that reason alone. In other words, I do not believe that one can fake it. A pastor cannot pretend to love the congregation so the congregation will accept what is being said.
>
> Love does not automatically establish all the connecting points for us, partly because biblical love is more commitment than sentiment and partly because it is not always easy to express love intelligently. But the Love of God—and our response of love one for another—does at least establish a crucial connecting point: We have to pay serious attention to how things affect people.[88]

What Wogaman says is true. We must live among the people, whose need for God is as fierce as their fears that he may not exist and that even if he does, he may have little interest in their hurts.

16. John Irving and John Hines both are clear on this matter of letting the preacher be a practitioner of life before he settles down to preach on it. John Irving said:

> The Reverend Mr. Wiggins' sermons were about as entertaining and convincing as a pilot's voice on the intercom, explaining technical difficulties while the plane plummets toward the earth and the stewardesses are screaming.[89]

John Hines said:

> Preaching is effective as long as the preacher expects something to happen—not because of the sermon, not even because of the preacher, but because of God.[90]

Preachers ought to live out their theories before they try them out on an audience. I recently heard a thirty-year-old preacher preach on human suffering. It didn't appear that he had ever suffered—even once. It seemed he had never even nicked himself while shaving.

those who need him and can't find him. He loves those whose quest for him is unrelenting, whose arguments with him are fierce.[15] You're generally writing *good* sermons, Sam. But you're not writing great ones."

"That's what Emma Johnson says."

"Listen to her, Sam. She could be sent by God."

"Yeah, or somebody else."

"All good sermons are well written. But great sermons— they have been lived before they are preached, and while the writing is important, nothing will put passion in a sermon like having lived it first.[16] For my part, I'd say we need to get back to where we first talked. I'd rather a preacher's manuscript be weaker than the need for God.

"So what about Emma's question, Sam. Do you love Jesus or not?" Sermoniel turned and his wings knocked a pile of books from the corner of Sam's desk.

"Hey, be careful, you celestial lummox!"

"Good word choice," said Sermoniel, turning back. This time his left wing nearly swept Sam's laptop computer off the desk.

"Hey, stop it!" Sam shouted.

"Well, all right! But if thou wouldst be great, work up an answer to Emma's question."

In a moment, Sermoniel was gone.

Sam laid down his ballpoint pen and switched on his

17. William Willimon said that the Bible "doesn't just want to preach to the modern world; it wants to convert it."[91] This notion of contemporaneity is behind Karl Barth's notion that we ought to preach with the Bible in one hand and the newspaper in the other.

Wayne McDill says:

> Michael Sack writes that Generation X, born between 1970 and 1985, is the feed-me generation who likes to retreat into small groups and needs unconditional acceptance and clear priorities. The Busters, born between 1960 and 1970, don't like guarantees, need relationships, peer philosophizing, and to become creatively involved in making a better world.[92]

Needless to say, these newer generations now add their cry for the "right now" sermon. In fact, "right now" sermons have always been in vogue. If a sermon is not right for right now, it has never worked in any era.

18. When an Episcopal bishop in America is presented his Bible, it is given to him with these words:

> Receive the Holy Scriptures. Feed the flock of Christ committed to your charge, guard and defend them in his truth, and be a faithful steward of his Holy Word and Sacraments. . . . Receive this Bible as a sign of his authority given unto you to preach the Word of God and to administer the Holy Sacraments. Do not forget the trust committed to you as a priest of the church of God. . . . Accept this Bible, and be among us as one who proclaims the Word. . . . Receive this book: here are the words of eternal life. Take them for your guide and declare them to the world. . . . Receive this book as a sign of the authority which God has given you this day to preach the Gospel of Christ and to minister his Holy Sacraments. . . . Give heed unto reading and unto exhortation and to doctrine. Think upon the things contained in this book. Be diligent in them that the increase thereby may be manifest unto all men. Take heed to thyself, and to doctrine, and be diligent in them; for in so doing thou shalt save both thyself and them that hear thee.[93]

Every pastor should emblazon this obligation on the sermon, for every sermon starts in the Bible and ends in the Bible or it can never call itself a sermon.

laptop. He had decided what his sermon would be on the next Sunday morning. He wrote, "No Compromise, or How to Stand in the Crisis." Then he roughed in some good sub-points: Luther at the Diet of Worms, Paul before Nero, Jesus before Pilate. He needed something contemporary: Janet Reno before the Waco–Branch-Davidian investigators. Mother Teresa at the National Prayer breakfast.[17] But he still needed a great story to finish the sermon up. He could think of nothing. What was on the old Norman Vincent Peale cassettes? Nothing. He went over his key-illustration file from *Preaching Today* cassettes. Zero! He bottomed out; he lowered himself to the lowest of all sermon sources and checked his e-mail illustrations. There he found one really funny story about three preachers who went fishing with a rabbi. He couldn't decide how to make it fit. The Holy Spirit, it seemed to him, rarely inhabited e-mail illustrations. He knew why John Updike once said that most of the stuff to be found on the information highway was roadkill.

It suddenly occurred to Sam that he had begun to think about sermon preparation totally in terms of the stories he needed to help him make his point. Without reference to either Jesus or the Bible. Could he actually do sermons this way?[18]

He decided he would preach on Daniel in the lions' den. Daniel was a perfect example of how to stand in the crisis. Besides, Daniel was an exotic character; everybody loved and

19. Word studies are an excellent way of doing what Richard Eslinger calls "breaking open a text." Often when we approach the sermon's text, it seems to be remote in content and we are hard pressed to find it significantly insightful. Then we begin to examine—with a lectionary or dictionary—the individual words of the text and find a richness that we missed on our first reading. We have found a way to "break it open," and we then find the richness of the text, wonderful truths we can pass on to our audience for their benefit. Once the words of the text have been made to yield their greatest truths, we can proceed to understand the text on many levels, and best of all, we can make the text—to use Eslinger's phrase—"mean something." Eslinger puts the importance of making the text meaningful this way:

> Perhaps we can also agree that Scripture is read first and foremost in the Sunday worship service for the community's edification. The preacher's role then is to preach from the scriptures that the laity have already welcomed and received as their own and do so in a way that sets each isolated beauty solidly within its proper context.[94]

20. Exhaustion is the mode of life for the parish pastor. The trick is how to work around it to be sure that our sermons inform and redeem the parishioners who are causing our exhaustion. To live in the midst of our congregation will inform us of their needs so that we can preach to them. It will also drain us to the point that we cannot address their needs with much vitality when it comes our turn to address them. Thompson reminds us:

> All pastoral preaching is intended to address the needs of the listeners. Much of our pastoral preaching has been focused on addressing either the immediate needs that the individuals express or the questions they ask. Preachers have little difficulty finding topics for preaching if they consistently preach in response to crises in the community or the personal crises of the people. The problem with such preaching is that it lacks any larger agenda for the preaching task.[95]

Preaching that rises within the congregation's needs is more likely to shut down the greater vision that a church might have, precisely because it becomes so parochial. But it is always interesting. The

feared lions. His old homiletics prof would be proud. He had arrived at his RNM, his rich narrative matrix, right on time. He looked the passage up! He ran through a word study. He felt so much better just having a text.[19]

Then he felt a chill. What if Sermoniel told Emma, his worst critic, about how long it took him to choose a text? They had taken to sitting together in church, and their friendship suddenly threatened him. If Sermoniel told Emma, she would tell the entire republic. He would never want Emma Johnson to know that he had outlined a whole sermon before he ever picked a text.

Sam was feeling pretty good about all his sermon preparation when the phone rang. An eleven-year-old girl—Judith Marie Thompson—from their Sunday school program had been struck by a car and died instantly.

Sam was devastated.

He quickly went to the hospital where the girl's family was still assembled. He spent the rest of the day there, and when the long draining evening had come to a close, Sam went home and fell into bed, exhausted.[20] He fell instantly to sleep and slept harder than he had in a long time.

Monday morning, the phone rang early. It was Mrs. Thompson wanting to know if Sam could meet with the funeral director to help make arrangements for Judith's memorial service. Of course he could. He got a second call

preacher's parish-exhaustion also shuts the preacher down, for there is nothing like fatigue to pull the margins of a great lifetime vision down to the fatiguing things that need to be taken care of in the moment.

21. These unanswerable and unending problems in the congregation can seem pointless and draining. What pastor does not have the feeling that the same few people are ever controlling his or her life? The problems of the people appear to be more like quicksand that sucks good homiletics into suffocation. But in reality, the problems of the people are the rich soil where biblical preaching becomes effective. Mark Barger Elliott writes:

> A pastoral preacher, in other words, begins with issues of the congregation clearly in mind. Harry Emerson Fosdick, a strong proponent of such preaching, wrote, "We need sermons that try to face people's real problems with them, meet their difficulties, answer their questions, confirm their most noble faiths, and interpret their experiences in sympathetic, wise, understanding co-operation." Fosdick believed the key to preaching effectively was understanding that preaching and personal counseling went hand in hand. William Willimon writes, "The leader of the liturgy will be most helpful to the community ... when it is apparent that the one who is the preacher in the pulpit and priest before the altar is also the pastor to the community."[96]

It may be hard to believe this in the midst of the unending shackles of human need, but it is nonetheless true. In serving as a parish pastor for more than thirty-five years, I am more convinced than ever that the best preachers are effective in front of large crowds because they have learned how to be effective in one-on-one encounters in the privacy of small human entanglements. After all, great preaching is just personal counseling done on a group basis.

22. Sam's sermon topic seemed good to him. But the truth is that sermons which focus on a crisis are not necessarily the best at focusing on God. In the average crisis, the crisis itself gets the attention God should have had. Helmut Thielicke said that during the bomb raids on Stuttgart he used to hear two kinds of prayers rising from the bomb shelters. Most prayed, "Lord, save us from the *bombs!*" and only a few prayed "*Lord,* save us from the bombs." Most believers cannot really

from his secretary at the church reminding him he was to meet with the Helwys couple at eleven. They were threatening to get a divorce. Good grief! Not again. They would probably never really get one, but they never stopped threatening.[21] Monday's pastoral calls continued through the day. On Monday night Sam fell into bed just as exhausted as he had been on Sunday.

Sam kept all of his Tuesday morning appointments and then had lunch with the chairman of the church board. That night he met again with Mrs. Helwys, who felt like she couldn't go on with her life. When Mrs. Helwys felt like she couldn't go on with her life, Sam couldn't get on with his very well either.

Monday and Tuesday were now gone. When Sam fell into bed that night, he realized he hadn't even thought about his unformed sermon, "How to Stand in the Crisis."[22] In fact, he felt he would be more comfortable lying down in a crisis. He was so exhausted that he dropped into bed. Wednesday, the Helwyses had a good day, but not the MacLemores. Susie MacLemore was at Deaconness Psychological Hospital suffering from marriage trauma. When Susie had trauma, so did Sam. After that call, Sam went back to the Thompsons to be sure they felt the support they needed. After attending a board meeting late that evening, Sam was very tired. The board had talked for the last four meetings about whether to replace the

get their minds on God when the crisis looms large. And preaching on a crisis will probably leave people talking more about the crisis than it leaves them talking about God. Wogaman writes:

> When the focus is entirely upon the sermon, it is more difficult for the sermon to focus on God. Worship draws us into something much larger than ourselves, reinforcing how the sermon must point beyond itself. When everything centers on the sermon, members of a worshiping congregation may feel this is quite normal, while at the same time many will feel a certain incompleteness.[97]

23. Sam's difficulty in being buried in the human struggles of his church should have provided for him a close look at reality. The congregation is there not to destroy the preacher's vitality but to provide the pastor a real vitality for preaching. Rick Ezell reminds us:

> Like a good teacher, Jesus started with the interests of his students and moved them toward the lessons he wanted to cover. Like a good salesperson, Christ started with the needs of the customers and not the product to be sold. Like a wise manager, Jesus began with the concerns of his employees and not His own agenda. He knew the exact location of his target audience, where they needed to go and what he had to do to help them get there.
>
> One can learn immensely from the methodology of Jesus. All Christian public speakers are wise to communicate spiritual truth by first discovering the needs of their target audience and then using this information as the starting point in their presentation.[98]

The thing that makes it difficult to let our target audience inform our preaching is that it often seems they are trying hard not to inform it but to stop it altogether.

24. It is difficult to work on pulpit passion in the consuming work of being pastor. It is difficult to seek Jesus when the people of the parish lay their crushing needs on you. Dostoyevsky is reported to have said that humanitarianism is just another form of atheism, for it takes the God-focus from us, replacing it with a focus on the needs of people. This has been a long-standing objection to the "social

piano in the children's wing. They were no closer to a resolution. But they were down to a three-to-three tie on Kawai versus Yamaha. It was after ten o'clock when Sam finally got home.

The message light on his phone was blinking. Should he answer it?[23] There were three calls waiting. He pushed the button to hear message 1: the Helwyses were not getting along as well as Sam had hoped. He pushed button 3 to delete the Helwyses. He loved deleting things.

The next call was even more demanding. Earl Payton had a hernia, and Ginger Payton wondered if he would mind helping Earl deal with it. She felt that Earl was questioning his faith: if God was just and loving, why would Earl have a hernia? Sam remembered only a year before when Earl questioned the justice of God because of his hemorrhoids. It seemed to Sam that anytime Earl had anything go wrong with his lower torso, he questioned the justice of God. He pushed button 3. Poof! There went Earl's hernia. He smiled; still, he made a note to stop by to see Earl on Thursday after the funeral.

The third call was from Emma Johnson, who still wanted to know if he loved Jesus and if he was praying about how to be more passionate.[24] Had he heard the evening news? There was trouble in Jerusalem. Could Dr. LeStraw be right about the Antichrist? He really should be reading Second Coming novels. "Watch for ye know not the hour." Sam looked at his

gospel." The assumption among seeker-sensitive churches is that people are seeking for God and that we can help them along. Willimon thinks otherwise:

> One of my problems with so-called seeker-sensitive churches is that, whatever most people are seeking, it isn't Jesus. We live in a society of omnivorous desire where people tend to grab at everything hoping that they might seize upon something that will give them a good reason to get out of bed in the morning. We are trained to be the relentless consumers who think that our lives can be made worthwhile through the acquisition of things. In such a climate it is too tempting for us preachers to reduce the Christian faith to just another lifestyle option, another means of making basically good people even better, another way to get what you thought you wanted before you wanted Jesus.[99]

Willimon is right and Wordsworth before him. Wordsworth wrote, "The world is too much with us; late and soon, / Getting and spending, we lay waste our powers." Congregational concern is the spending of all our emotional resources. We can purchase wisdom at this expense, but we cannot purchase pulpit passion. Passion comes only from wanting the right thing: Jesus and the fullness of his presence in our hearts.

25. Saturday is indeed a blessed day! It is the last-chance day. For the disciplined pastor, it is the day of polishing what has been written. For the harried pastor, it is a day of patching enough stuff together to actually preach come Sunday. John Killinger offers this word for Saturday:

> It is important . . . to complete the written sermon by Thursday or Friday in order to permit time for the familiarization process. David H. C. Read says that he normally finishes writing by noon on Friday. He reads over his manuscript that afternoon, and again on Saturday, time permitting. Then on Saturday night he gives it a serious reading, attempting to see the sermon as a whole and to be able to reconstruct it in his mind. He does not try to memorize it, only to try and see it in its general shape. On Sunday morning he gives it a final reading and rethinks it as he walks to church.[100]

There is something wonderful and idyllic in Read's discipline. But one wonders if it worked out that way very often. Most preachers rarely

watch. The hour was late. *Jesus*, he thought prayerfully, *come whenever you want, but please don't let Emma be right*. Sam thought of all the weekend work that lay ahead and prayed, *Lord, come on Saturday . . . early, if you don't mind*.

Wednesday! The week was half over and Wednesday was entirely over. Sam collapsed into bed. He slept until the Thursday-morning sun streamed through his window waking him to his duties. Sam studied all morning and attended the missionary women's tea that afternoon. They were discussing the importance of work among the Watusi. Sam knew it was certainly important to the women and probably to the Watusi. They would want him there. He went. That night, Sam was so tired he never even thought of "How to Stand in the Crisis."

Friday was a blur with four more unscheduled counseling appointments, and suddenly it was Saturday night.[25] What had happened to Friday? It was at his bedroom desk that Sam got earnest about the unfinished work of Sunday. In horror, he turned his attention to his sermon and had just opened his hard drive with his computer mouse when the phone rang.

"Pastor Sam," began the plaintive voice.

It was Luella Parsons. Sam knew her meek little voice. She had never called him once to inquire after his well-being. Blueberry strudel was her only real life achievement.

"Yes, this is Pastor Sam. Is this Luella?"

carry such a clean sermon agenda against the mayhem of their congregational work. Most of the time Saturday night is catch-up and clean-up sermon time and not a time for the leisurely work of looking at the brilliant literature the preacher has already produced for the pulpit come Sunday morning.

26. Wogaman writes:

> I have written . . . of the pastoral context as though it were simply a relationship of a pastor to the people whom he or she is called to serve. That relationship is very real and very important. But a pastoral relationship must not be seen as exclusively one-on-one. It is a quality of community life. Indeed, no pastor can keep up alone with the personal needs of a whole congregation, unless the group is very small. Even then the quality of Christian love is undermined if the love is not in some sense communal, people in the congregation caring about each other, a care that spills over into the world beyond the church. A care giving congregation is a marvelous seedbed for genuinely prophetic preaching.[101]

Once again this statement is too ideal, for even the most caring congregation will often pile such woes upon their caregiver that all his quest for pulpit passion will have been destroyed by the people he feels called to care for.

27. A true man of God! Isn't that the goal to which we all aspire? But we don't feel like true men of God. Often our trip into the pulpit is prefaced by "Why me?" instead of "Thus sayeth the Lord!" The best men and women of God are the last to call themselves that. Nor would they ever feel comfortable calling their homilies by so grand a title as the Word of God. Ron Allen speaks for all of us when he says:

> I vividly remember sitting in the chancel before my first sermon. I was an undergraduate student in the College of the Bible at Phillips University. I was invited to fill the pulpit of my home church one summer Sunday while our pastor was on vacation. My heart was beating so hard I could feel it in my chest. My palms sweat. My mouth was dry. I began to shake. I wondered whether I could stand and speak. . . . On the one hand the community supported me. I could see it in their eyes. I could feel it

"Yes, Sam. Sam, you know I am not one to beat around the bush."

"Yes, that's true, Luella."

"Well, I heard that you told Earl Payton that hernias are not sent by God, and now he's real confused over where it came from. Now Sam, if God didn't send that hernia, where did it come from?"

"It comes from a weakness in the abdominal wall, Luella. You just shouldn't look for spiritual reasons for every little hiccup and hernia."

"Sam! I'm surprised at you. Where's your heart, pastor? Don't you love Jesus?"[26]

"Luella, sometimes bad things happen to good people. Oh, Luella, let's all go to sleep. We can talk about Earl's hernia in the morning, okay?"

"Go to sleep! Go to sleep! Could you not watch with me one hour! I'll tell you this, Pastor Sam, I'm going over to the Methodist church in the morning. Brother Jones is their pastor. He's a true man of God! He knows where hernias come from."[27]

Sam shuddered, then he shot out an unguarded word: "Yeah, and I've heard that you don't make your strudel from scratch. Is it true? Do you start with a mix, Luella?"

"What did you say, Sam? What did you say?" Sam could hear the heat rising in Luella's voice. He decided not to repeat what he had said.

in their handshakes. On the other hand, speaking on behalf of God invoked a heavier responsibility than giving an informative talk in speech class ... even the most seasoned preachers have such anxieties.[102]

28. One of those weeks! How do you bless the congregation when they have been most requiring? We shall name God Lord, even when the requirements of the Word seem brutal to us. Wogaman asks the question for us:

> How shall we name God? By what name shall we know God? For the ancient Hebrews that was a difficult question. God the ineffable majesty. God the power in whose destiny, in whose life, we find our destiny. God who controls the circumstances of human existence. How shall we name God? The one we approach in prayer.[103]

Out of gas. Out of joy. Out of passion. There is only one place we may go: to the God of empowering presence, the God of beginning again, the God of prayer.

29. We are brought to the ragged edge by the feeling there is a huge gap between the Christ we believe in as preachers and the one our members seem to demonstrate in their treatment of us. Frank Honeycutt illustrates:

> In a recent installment of "Kudzu" in the Sunday comics, Pulitzer-prize winning cartoonist Doug Marlette depicts the Reverend Will B. Dunn addressing his congregation from the pulpit. The preacher is grinning and waving a piece of paper in the opening panel. He looks out over the top of his glasses and says to his flock, "Okay Gang! Pop Quiz!" The Reverend Will B. Dunn is obviously pleased with himself and says to his flock, "Brothers and sisters," he says, "Today I want to give you a test—a spiritual maturity test. This test will measure your depth of spiritual development as a congregation. Okay, ready? First question—Complete the sentence: 'Whosoever shall smite ye on your right cheek ...'" And without hesitation the congregation thunders back. "WASTE 'EM! SUE HIS CARCASS! STRING 'IM UP!" The last panel shows a depressed Reverend thinking these words to himself: "I may be forced to grade on the curve."[104]

"Luella, it's late! Go to bed!"

Sam heard the phone click. He had lost his temper. Why had he been so brash? Like Moses he had struck the strudel of God. It could be costly. Now he must stand on Nebo and watch Luella enter the Promised Land. Sam knew he needed to take important stands, die for important issues, and Luella's strudel was not a great hill to die on.

It had been one of those weeks.[28]

The Paytons would take their theological hernia to the Methodist church, and Luella Parsons would no doubt be baking her blueberry strudel in a new denominational arena. Sam couldn't think why he had ever thought he wanted to preach on how to stand in a crisis. His mind was too fried to work on the sermon; he decided he would go to bed and get up early on Sunday morning to try to get his thoughts together on the subject. He was living on the ragged edge.[29]

Sam had a wretched night of sleep. He found himself floating in a pink ether, and he seemed to drift like a feather into the final scene of time. There were God and Earl Payton talking. One of the Seraphim flew through the heavens crying, "Behold the great Hernia of Heaven." There was Earl girt about the loins with a velcro truss. He was wearing a halo, and all the beasts and elders fell on their faces when Earl passed before them. There was Emma Johnson too. She was holding a Second Coming novel in her left hand, and in her right hand

30. Preachers realize that sermons are sermons precisely because they rely on the fact that the Bible has something to say. "The Bible says" is the secret of our authority, and it rings with an authority that we should be honest about. William Willimon says:

> There may be religions that begin with long walks in the woods, communing with nature, getting close to trees. There may be religions that delve into the recesses of a person's ego, rummaging around in the psyche. Christianity is not one of those religions.
>
> Here is a people who begin with the action of taking up the scroll, being confronted with stories of God, stories that insert themselves into our accustomed way of doing business and challenge us to change or else be out of step with the way things are now that God has entered into human history.
>
> They hand Jesus the scroll. He reads from the prophet Isaiah, speaking of that day when God would again act to set things right, to come for Israel, to lift up the downtrodden and push down the mighty. The Spirit of the Lord is upon them to announce God's advent.[105]

When Jesus took up the scroll in the Nazarene synagogue, he symbolized the authority of the sermon and fixed it for all preachers everywhere. No wonder, then, that Sam could count on saying "the Bible says" to work evangelical and homiletic magic even if he was abusing the symbol.

she held a great book titled *How to Have Passion in Preaching*. Sam was suddenly ashamed that he had been so insensitive to Emma. There were great herds of sheep and goats, and the goats all wore little neckbands that read, "Goats who told people they were sheep!" Sam was stunned! He was standing with the goats!

When he woke up, it was 6 A.M. on Sunday morning. He hurriedly dressed and dashed off to his study at church to begin the sermon he had not yet finished. When he got there, his mind was dead. Nothing came to him. Unless some miracle occurred, he would never finish writing "How to Stand in a Crisis." He had only two or three choices. The first and worst was simply to stand up and admit he had no sermon. This would, of course, never do. The second was to fake it. This he could do. He had done it before. He had learned how to say very little with a great deal of flair. The key was to look intent, quote three hymn texts, and tell what they meant to his mother. He had discovered that no one would attack his sermon when he spoke about his mother. He had found the key to sermonless preaching. One had to keep the voice level up and say "the Bible says" a lot.[30] But usually he found that this was unconvincing to those who had heard him when he was better prepared. The third choice was to preach an old sermon, one so old that those who had already heard it might not notice they were hearing it again.

31. Allen reveals a conversation he overheard between two desperate students who had "Saturday night fever":

> Pat: "So, what are you preaching this Sunday?"
>
> Chris: "Well . . . uh . . . ah . . . oh . . . hmm . . ."
>
> Pat: "I don't know either. I'll look at the lectionary. Some of the folks want me to do a sermon on the family. I could turn some of the lectures in my psalms course into a sermon series."
>
> Chris: "How will you decide? I mean this is Friday, and you've got to preach on Sunday. Maybe you have the power to keep Sunday from coming but I don't. For me, the hardest part of sermon preparation is deciding what to preach about."
>
> Pat: "Yeah. Sometimes I sit for hours in front of a blank computer screen, my mind as blank as the screen."
>
> Experienced preachers typically find it easier to settle on a starting point for a sermon. However, even experienced pastors need to evaluate their options for developing a sermon for a particular Sunday so that the sermon and the occasion are mutually appropriate.[106]

The key to vital sermons is to steep oneself in the material to be preached and live within the sermon till it is complete. If the preacher walks for a week or more in the midst of what is to be preached, he or she is less likely to come down to Saturday night dreading Sunday.

32. The congregation loves nothing better than a preacher who confesses his utter need for God. That need openly confesses that we would like to get our sermon texts from our private affair with God, and then we would like to be sure that the text is bathed in our need to present it just as God wants it said. Douglas White said this:

> While there will be a prayerful attitude all the way through, that the Spirit of God shall overshadow all of our preparatory activities, there must be that final turning of the whole thing over to God. Mind and heart must always be coordinated. When we feel that we have a firsthand grasp of the truth contained in the passage under consideration, we need to get on our knees and ask God to put fire into our facts. The slogan of one Christian institution is "Knowledge on Fire." We must pray that God will make the truth which he has revealed to our minds a living thing in our hearts, and a reality in our own expe-

"Jesus," he prayed, "Emma Johnson wants to know if I love you. I need to know that too. I've worn myself out being a pastor, and Sermoniel says that one of the places that passion is to be found is among the people. I've looked there all week, Lord, and never found you. The other place is in the silence, and there hasn't been much of that in my life this week, Lord. Help me!"

"Ahem!" said a voice behind him. It was Sermoniel. "Excuse me, did you want help so you could bring God to the people or merely to keep you from looking bad when the hungry sheep show up here in a couple of hours?"[31]

"Don't get philosophical with me, Sermoniel. I'm a desperate man!"

"Frankly, Sam, you must remember what I told you long ago—back before your church began to grow. Most people will not long tolerate preaching that is more tied to the preacher's preparation than to his need for God.[32] Sam, do you need God?"

"Like right now!"

"Yes, like right now! And I'm not asking if you need him just to keep you from homiletic failure."

Sam stretched. The air in the room was stifling, much heavier than he wanted it to be.

"Sam," Sermoniel said, "the bishop's headgear is referred to as a mitre. It is in the shape of a flame, so neither the

rience, for only then can we hope to preach convincingly and powerfully. To carry on traffic in unfelt truth is a dangerous and unprofitable undertaking.[107]

33. Bernard of Clairvaux, *Selected Works*.[108]

34. How important is the Sabbath? Swindoll calls it the Holy Spirit's churning place:

> I think that the Spirit of God is doing many things he never gets credit for. To start with, I think he prompts ideas and prepares the soil of our souls for certain subjects. I felt that was true—definitely true—in my series on grace that led to *The Grace Awakening*. There were some things that we'd gone through that created some growing feelings—churnings within. We all have what I call a "churning place." That's not an original thought with me, but I have used those words which I got from another. I think the Spirit churns us—he prompts us—and in that process, I believe he begins to build the steam in our areas of motivation and instill a growing sense of passion.[109]

Sabbaths are places where we create a stillness, but it can result in a powerful homiletic churning, a churning which God creates and from which he forms his Word for our congregations.

35. Unless the Bible is doing things in the preacher's life, merely finding a text he or she can preach to others will accomplish nothing. Perhaps the greatest thing wrong with preaching the Bible is that the preacher has merely hawked the Scriptures to the crowd, having let it pass through the preacher without affecting him. John MacArthur wisely observes:

> I must measure my own life before God. I must first of all be a man of God. What I say is the overflow of who I am. I will never be powerful in the pulpit if I am not speaking out of the vortex of a dynamic relationship with the living God. That is where it starts.
>
> The measure of my ministry is this: Was I a steward of the mysteries of God? Did I guard the treasure so that from the beginning to the end of my life I kept the purity of truth? Did I faithfully proclaim the truth as it should be proclaimed? These are the marks of a faithful steward.
>
> I am so passionately burdened not to misinterpret Scripture. I am driven by my understanding of Scripture. It drives

bishop nor the church will ever forget that it is the Spirit who descends on the church with that power of transformation that no amount of sermon crafting can ever furnish the sermon."

"But I have been among the people all week; if God can be found among the people, why am I so dry this morning?"

"God cannot be found among the people until he has first been found in the silence. Mark this down, Sam: you can't help people if you're always with people. You must first find God in the silence if you want to find him among the people. Bernard of Clairvaux also said, 'Waiting upon God is not idleness, but work which beats all other work to one unskilled in it.'[33] The passion that it takes to make the sermon work is missing because you are unskilled at the work of waiting."

Sam held his face in his hands a long time.

It was true he had no sermon.

But he could see that the answer was not to panic in scratching out some hurried sermon substitute. The answer was to create a Sabbath, and it was not too late for one. It was never too late to create a Sabbath.[34] There were still two hours till church time, and it was a good time for quiet. He closed his eyes and held his hands out in a gesture of need.

He knew not how long he remained in this posture, but he was gradually aware of the arrival of some cars in the parking lot outside. Romans 8:28 came to him, not as a sermon text but as a pillar of fire in the darkness.[35]

everything in my life, because I take the psalmist's statement to be true when he said in Psalm 138:2, "For you have exalted above all things your name and your word." Nothing is more precious to God than his Word, and every time I interpret a passage, I exercise a sacred trust. I'm driven by that, compelled to be a steward of that treasure and to regard it with all the faculties and spiritual resources that I have.[110]

36. Brown Taylor observes the importance of taking the time to live in the presence of God:

Down in the darkness below those dreams—in the place where our notions about God have come to naught—there is still reason to hope, because disillusionment is not so bad. Disillusionment is the loss of illusion—about ourselves, about the world, about God—and while it is almost always painful, it is not a bad thing to lose the lies we have mistaken for the truth. Disillusioned, we come to understand that God does not always conform to our expectations. We glimpse our own relative size in the universe and see that no human being can say how God should be or how God should act. We review our requirement of God and recognize them as our own fictions, our own frail shelter against the vast night sky.[111]

Only when we agree to massive doses of time alone with God can we ever come to understand both our significance and insignificance to God.

37. Sermons are the servants of grace, and homiletically speaking, grace is the dispensation of hope. Whatever else a sermon should do, it must serve grace by dispensing hope. Wogaman writes:

Prophetic preaching deals not only with problems and evils to be overcome; it offers hope that they can be overcome. This was the hallmark of most of the great biblical prophets, and it has been a striking contribution of the African-American pulpit. No matter how wretched the situation may be, no matter how powerful the forces of evil that confront us, no matter how futile all aspirations may seem—still, nevertheless, it is God's world, so there is always hope.[112]

Minutes later, he walked into the pulpit.

"Today," said Sam, "I have no sermon, but I do have a text." He quoted Romans 8:28 and then Julian of Norwich. "God wants you to know how much he loves you, and he wants you to know that what you now carry is a burden he wishes to take from you." He turned first to Emma Johnson, and without ever using her name, he proceeded to answer her question. "I have been urged to answer the question as to whether I love Jesus. I discovered this week that it takes time to love Jesus, and I have not spent the time required to do it."[36] His confession was rooted in five minutes of evidence that he had found no love-seeking Sabbath till that very morning. But he pledged himself to the keeping of such Sabbaths.

Then as his eyes swept past the Helwyses, Sam said that all would be well. Their eyes met and the single look was a sacrament of healing. None but the Helwyses felt the weight of the glory. "Yes, all will be well. For all who suffer damaged relationships can start again. That's what grace is; it's the land of beginning again.[37] Let none who quarrel ever state their positions to win or concede," said Sam. "We must all begin at the silence of the throne. Take your wounded marriages to God. Don't try to be right or prove anyone else wrong. Just sit in the silence. All shall be well if the starting point is well."

Then he saw Earl Payton. He made no attempt to define Earl's problem as one of little significance. It was clear that it

38. John MacArthur has continually reminded us that our sufficiency is Christ and has prided himself on the fact that while the Bible
is the heartbeat of his ministry, Jesus is its focus. Considering Christ-
centered preaching, he says:

> That's why I wrote my book *Our Sufficiency in Christ*. . . . I don't
> think we begin to realize just how bad our current situation is
> until we detect how little interest there is in pursuing Christ.[113]

39. The miracle that is central in preaching is that one man speaking in behalf of God could convince other men that they should hear
any message and respond to it by changing. People change when one
man or woman convinces others that their face-to-face sermonic
encounter holds the glory of grace passing from preacher to church
attendee for the sake of the attendee and the God who is calling the
world to personal transformation. Henry Ward Beecher wrote more
than one hundred years ago:

> You put a man in one of those barreled pulpits, where there is
> no responsibility laid upon him as to his body, and he falls into
> all manner of gawky attitudes, and rests himself like a country
> horse at a hitching post. He sags down, and has no con-
> sciousness of his awkwardness. But bring him out on a plat-
> form and see how much more manly he becomes, how much
> more force comes out. The moment a man is brought face to
> face with other men, then does the influence of each act and
> react upon the other.[114]

was significant to Earl. "All shall be well, even when God seems absent or when we cannot find his presence. Never poke around in your resentment to bring God to trial. Rather, sit in the silence, and lay aside your question. It is your doubt that makes you poor. But God is richer than your poverty."

The Thompsons were there, numbed by the death of their child. Sam held up his text to them and invited them to the Sabbath of God's rich inclusion.

"I've no major answers to your need. Great loss knows only one source of sufficiency.[38] Sometimes we find no solace because there is no solace. When there are no answers, God himself is the answer. Come to his Sabbath. I'll meet you there. All shall be well and all shall be well and all manner of things shall be well."

Emma hadn't noticed that Sermoniel was sitting beside her till the sermon was over. She had no idea how long he had been there.

"I see you're back in services this Sunday," she said.

"I had to come today," Sermoniel said. "I always like seeing how preachers behave when they don't have a sermon."

"Oh, but he did have a sermon!"

"Yeah! But not the three-points-and-a-poem kind."

"But when anyone convinces me to have a go at God, I think that's preaching![39] This morning his sermon did what sermons ought to do: Sam became God's conduit to the center

40. While it may be dangerous to see emotion as the only way of measuring a sermon's effectiveness, certainly the lack of feeling often prevalent in churches must condemn many pulpiteers of misunderstanding its importance. Emotion is a life sign, a symbol that the sermon is being heard. It is even a sign that the sermon's auditors are involved and being challenged to meet God with whatever demands he may be laying on them. Whatever else it may say, emotion shouts, "I feel. I am involved." David Mulder wisely observes:

> Much of the Church Growth research published in the past decade indicates that an emotional event is the primary catalyst for changing lives. People most often join a church or drop away from a church during an emotion-charged change in their lives. These "emotional events" range from moving into a new home or community to losing a job and finding a new one, from welcoming a new baby into a household to facing a life-threatening illness.
>
> Individuals who join a church because of an emotional event naturally expect to be emotionally impacted in worship. A story or narrative sermon is an excellent way to make an emotional connection between their lives and God's Word. Stories touch the heart as well as the head, and, by the power of the Holy Spirit, they touch the will of the listener. When the will of a person is touched, action occurs—change happens.[115]

of our need. Sam invited us to sit down with him inside his heart, and he held his exposed soul out to us as an altar. He has learned the priestly function of a preacher. Our need and God's supply must always meet in the sermon, or there is no sermon. Oh no, you're quite wrong, sir. That was a sermon, for each of us in Sam's pulpit words met with the Almighty and life seems bearable."

"But what about your question? Does he love Jesus? Did he preach with passion?"

"Look at him, sir."

Sermoniel did. There were lots of people clustered around Sam. Some of them looked like they were weeping.

"See!" Emma said. "Look at all those people. I think he spoke to them; what do you think?"[40]

The Angel of Homiletics didn't answer, but he was smiling. Then his smile widened to a grin as he faded from sight. Only the grin remained. It seemed to move from its place in the pew and then floated forward till it hovered over Sam as though it approved of his very honest sermon. It lingered for just a moment and then . . .

Then even the grin was gone.

"Stop doing that!" said Emma.

But no matter! Whenever God smiles on good preaching, all angels are obligated to grin.

NOTES

1. James L. Crenshaw, *Trembling at the Threshold of a Biblical Text* (Grand Rapids: Eerdmans, 1994), 14.
2. John R. W. Stott, *Between Two Worlds: The Art of Preaching in the Twentieth Century* (Grand Rapids: Eerdmans, 1982), 283.
3. Keith Willhite, *Preaching with Relevance* (Grand Rapids: Kregel, 2001), 131.
4. Barbara Brown Taylor, *When God Is Silent* (Boston: Cowley Publications, 1998), 51.
5. Bill Hybels, "Speaking to the Secular Mind," *Leadership* (summer 1988), 29–30.
6. Phillips Brooks, *On Preaching* (New York: Seabury, 1964), 170.
7. Willhite, *Preaching with Relevance,* 129.
8. Hugh Litchfield, *Visualizing the Sermon* (Sioux Falls, S.Dak.: Hugh Litchfield, 1996), 13.
9. Os Guinness, *The Call* (Nashville: Word, 1998), 117, quoting William Golding, *The Spire.*
10. Brown Taylor, *When God Is Silent,* 85.
11. Calvin Miller, "The Twenty-Day Sermon," from *When the Aardvark Parked on the Ark* (San Francisco: Harper and Row, 1984), 133.
12. Crenshaw, *Trembling at the Threshold,* 104.
13. Kenton C. Anderson, *Preaching with Conviction* (Grand Rapids: Kregel, 2001), 76.
14. Guinness, *The Call,* 4.
15. Donald W. McCullough, *The Trivialization of God: The Dangerous Illusion of a Manageable Deity* (Colorado Springs: NavPress, 1995), 77.
16. James William McClendon Jr., *Biography as Theology* (Nashville: Abingdon, 1974), 37.
17. James Houston, *The Transforming Friendship: A Guide to Prayer* (Oxford: Lion, 1989), 11.
18. Klaus Issler, *Wasting Time with God* (Downers Grove, Ill.: InterVarsity, 2001), 14.
19. Ernest Becker, *The Denial of Death* (New York: The Free Press, 1973), 90.
20. Issler, *Wasting Time with God,* 26.
21. Guinness, *The Call,* 61.
22. Harry Emerson Fosdick, *The Living of These Days* (New York: Harper and Brothers, 1956), 100.
23. Alister McGrath, *A Passion for Truth* (Downers Grove, Ill.: InterVarsity, 1996), 55.

24. Calvin Miller, *Spirit, Word, and Story* (Grand Rapids: Baker, 1996), 96.

25. Ibid., 92.

26. Ibid., 53.

27. Crenshaw, *Trembling at the Threshold,* 28.

28. Stott, *Between Two Worlds,* 144.

29. Calvin Miller, *A Covenant for All Seasons* (Wheaton: Shaw, 1995), xiii.

30. Allan Bloom, *The Closing of the American Mind* (New York: Simon and Schuster, 1987), 60.

31. Eugene Lowry, *The Sermon* (Nashville: Abingdon, 1997), 31.

32. Brown Taylor, *When God Is Silent,* 22.

33. Willhite, *Preaching with Relevance,* 131.

34. Litchfield, *Visualizing the Sermon,* 17.

35. Brown Taylor, *When God Is Silent,* 73.

36. Guinness, *The Call,* 35.

37. John Killinger, *Fundamentals of Preaching* (Minneapolis: Fortress Press, 1996), 47.

38. Ibid., 47–48.

39. Charles L. Campbell, *Preaching Jesus* (Grand Rapids: Eerdmans, 1997), 130–31.

40. William R. Bouknight, *The Authoritative Word* (Nashville: Abingdon, 2001), 71.

41. Campbell, *Preaching Jesus,* xi.

42. Ibid.

43. Michael Duduit, *Communicate with Power: Insights from America's Top Communicators* (Grand Rapids: Baker, 1996), 222–24.

44. Killinger, *Fundamentals of Preaching,* 15.

45. Gustav Wingren, *Luther on Vocation* (Philadelphia: Fortress Press, 1957), 72.

46. John MacArthur, *Rediscovering Expository Preaching* (Dallas: Word, 1992), 340–41.

47. Calvin Miller, *Marketplace Preaching* (Grand Rapids: Baker, 1995), 151.

48. Warren Wiersbe, *Preaching and Teaching with Imagination* (Grand Rapids: Baker, 1994), 58.

49. Miller, *Spirit, Word, and Story,* 218.

50. David L. Larsen, *Telling the Old, Old Story* (Wheaton: Crossway, 1995), 73–74.

51. Miller, *Spirit, Word, and Story,* 153.

52. Charles Swindoll, *The Tardy Oxcart* (Nashville: Word, 1998), xvi.

53. Marsh Cassady, *Acting Step-by-Step* (San Jose: Resource Publications, 1988), 2.

54. W. E. Sangster, *The Craft of Sermon Construction* (London: Pickering, 1984), 24.

55. Frank G. Honeycutt, *Preaching to Skeptics and Seekers* (Nashville: Abingdon, 2001), 25.

56. Keith Nickle, *Preaching the Gospel of Luke* (Louisville: Westminster John Knox, 2000), 221.

57. Miller, *Spirit, Word, and Story,* 120.

58. Leanne Payne, *Real Presence* (Grand Rapids: Baker, 1995), 103.

59. Craig Loscalzo, *Evangelistic Preaching That Connects* (Downers Grove, Ill.: InterVarsity, 1995), 27.

60. James W. Thompson, *Preaching Like Paul* (Louisville: Westminster John Knox, 2001), 121.

61. Barbara Brown Taylor, *The Luminous Web* (Cambridge, Mass.: Cowley Press, 2000), 3.

62. Donald Coggan, *Preaching: The Sacrament of the Word* (New York: Crossroads, 1988), 75.

63. William Willimon, *Peculiar Speech: Preaching to the Baptized* (Grand Rapids: Eerdmans, 1992), 2.

64. David Buttrick, *Speaking Parables: A Homiletic Guide* (Louisville: Westminster John Knox, 2000), xiii.

65. Miller, *Spirit, Word, and Story,* 159, quoting Bruno Bettelheim.

66. Ibid., 171, quoting F. Dean Lueking.

67. Ibid, quoting Allan Bloom.

68. Calvin Miller, *The Empowered Communicator* (Nashville: Broadman and Holman, 1994), 112, quoting F. Scott Fitzgerald.

69. Richard L. Eslinger, *Pitfalls in Preaching* (Grand Rapids: Eerdmans, 1996), 131.

70. David Buttrick, *A Captive Voice* (Louisville: John Knox, 1994), 47.

71. J. Philip Wogaman, *Speaking the Truth in Love* (Louisville: Westminster John Knox, 1998), 75.

72. David P. Mulder, *Narrative Preaching* (St. Louis: CPH Publishing, 1973), 11.

73. Coggan, *Preaching,* 159.

74. Rick Ezell, *Hitting a Moving Target* (Kregel: Grand Rapids, 1999), 87.

75. Buttrick, *Speaking Parables,* xiv.

76. Coggan, *Preaching,* 75.

77. Nickle, *Preaching the Gospel of Luke,* 141.

78. Anna Akhmatova, *Selected Poems,* trans. D. M. Thomas (New York: Penguin, 1976), 122.

79. Ezell, *Hitting a Moving Target,* 49.

80. Mark Barger Elliott, *Creative Styles of Preaching* (Louisville: Westminster John Knox, 2000), 150.

81. Thompson, *Preaching Like Paul,* 41.

82. Coggan, *Preaching,* 84.

83. Elliott, *Creative Styles of Preaching,* 19.

84. Bouknight, *Authoritative Word,* 77.

85. Coggan, *Preaching,* 95.

86. Bouknight, *Authoritative Word,* 53.

87. Thompson, *Preaching Like Paul,* 85.

88. Wogaman, *Speaking the Truth in Love,* 19, 47.

89. *Quotes for the Journey, Wisdom for the Way,* ed. Gordon S. Jackson (Colorado Springs: NavPress, 2000), 131.

90. Ibid.

91. Ezell, *Hitting a Moving Target,* 45.

92. Wayne McDill, *Moment of Truth* (Nashville: Broadman and Holman, 1999), 45.

93. Coggan, *Preaching,* 21–22.

94. Eslinger, *Pitfalls in Preaching,* 35.

95. Thompson, *Preaching Like Paul,* 90.

96. Elliott, *Creative Styles of Preaching*, 108–9.
97. Wogaman, *Speaking the Truth in Love*, 29.
98. Ezell, *Hitting a Moving Target*, 85.
99. William H. Willimon, foreword to *Preaching to Skeptics and Seekers*, by Frank. G. Honeycutt (Nashville: Abingdon, 2001), 11.
100. Killinger, *Fundamentals of Preaching*, 166.
101. Wogaman, *Speaking the Truth in Love*, 23.
102. Ronald Allen, *Interpreting the Gospel* (St. Louis: Chalice Press, 1998), 1.
103. Wogaman, *Speaking the Truth in Love*, 128.
104. Honeycutt, *Preaching to Skeptics and Seekers*, 111.
105. Willimon, *Peculiar Speech*, 19.
106. Allen, *Interpreting the Gospel*, 99.
107. Douglas M. White, *The Excellence of Exposition* (Neptune, N.J.: Lozeaux Brothers, 1977), 100.
108. Bernard of Clairvaux, *Selected Works*, trans. G. R. Evans (Mahwah, N.J.: Paulist Press, 1987), 63.
109. Duduit, *Communicate with Power*, 193–94.
110. Ibid., 129–30.
111. Barbara Brown Taylor, *The Preaching Life* (Cambridge, Mass.: Cowley Publications, 1993), 8.
112. Wogaman, *Speaking the Truth in Love*, 82.
113. Duduit, *Communicate with Power*, 127.
114. McDill, *Moment of Truth*, 95.
115. Mulder, *Narrative Preaching*, 26.